The Federal Government

THE JUDICIAL BRANCH

Interpreting America's Laws

Hamed Madani, Ph.D.

MyReportLinks.com Books
an imprint of

Enslow Publishers, Inc. **E**
Box 398, 40 Industrial Road
Berkeley Heights, NJ 07922
USA

MyReportLinks.com Books, an imprint of Enslow Publishers, Inc. MyReportLinks®
is a registered trademark of Enslow Publishers, Inc.

Library of Congress Cataloging-in-Publication Data

Madani, Hamed.
 The judicial branch : interpreting America's laws / Hamed Madani.
   p. cm. — (The federal government)
 Includes bibliographical references and index.
ISBN-13: 978-1-59845-059-0
ISBN-10: 1-59845-059-X
 1. United States. Supreme Court—Juvenile literature. 2. Courts—United States—Juvenile
literature. I. Title.
  KF8700.Z9.M34 2007
  347.73'26—dc22

                                    2006023963

Printed in the United States of America

10 9 8 7 6 5 4 3 2 1

To Our Readers:
Through the purchase of this book, you and your library gain access to the Report Links that specifically back up this book.
The Publisher will provide access to the Report Links that back up this book and will keep these Report Links up to date on **www.myreportlinks.com** for five years from the book's first publication date.
We have done our best to make sure all Internet addresses in this book were active and appropriate when we went to press. However, the author and the Publisher have no control over, and assume no liability for, the material available on those Internet sites or on other Web sites they may link to.
The usage of the MyReportLinks.com Books Web site is subject to the terms and conditions stated on the Usage Policy Statement on **www.myreportlinks.com.**
A password may be required to access the Report Links that back up this book. The password is found on the bottom of page 4 of this book.
Any comments or suggestions can be sent by e-mail to comments@myreportlinks.com or to the address on the back cover.

♻ Enslow Publishers, Inc., is committed to printing our books on recycled paper. The paper in every book contains 10% to 30% post-consumer waste (PCW). The cover board on the outside of each book contains 100% PCW. Our goal is to do our part to help young people and the environment too!

Photo Credits: ACLU, p. 110; Administrative Office of the U.S. Courts, p. 19; Alliance for Justice, p. 116; APVA Preservation Virginia, p. 54; AP/Wide World Photos, pp. 90, 94; Black Box Voting, p. 112; Columbia University, p. 81; © Corel Corporation, pp. 1, 3, 8–9, 22–23, 32–33, 114–115; Cornell Law School, p. 107; Doug Linder, Professor of Law/University of Missouri-Kansas City Law School, p. 100; Enslow Publishers, Inc., p. 5; Evisum, p. 76; Federal Judicial Center, p. 52; FindLaw, p. 40; First Federal Congress Project, p. 102; Gerhard Peters—Americanpresidency.org, p. 11; Juan Williams, p. 69; Library of Congress, pp. 58, 59, 62–63, 67, 77, 80, 83, 85, 96, 104–105; MyReportLinks.com Books, p. 4; National Archives, p. 108; National Cable Satellite Corporation, p. 15; National Center for State Courts, p. 13; OYEZ, p. 65; Painting by John Beale Bordley, 1836, p. 56; PBS, p. 61; Photos.com, pp. 27–28, 36; Ronald Reagan Presidential Library, pp. 73, 88; Shutterstock.com, pp. 6, 7, 49, 97; Supreme Court of the United States, pp. 29, 91; The College of William and Mary, p. 71; The Supreme Court Historical Society, pp. 38, 87; The White House, pp. 12, 16, 74; Time, Inc., p. 78; United States Court of Appeals for the Federal Circuit, p. 34; United States Tax Court, p. 48; USAVC/U.S. Court of Appeals for Veterans Claims, p. 44; U.S. Court of Appeals for the Armed Forces/U.S. Courts, p. 42; U.S. Court of Federal Claims/U.S. Courts, p. 45; U.S. Court of International Trade/U.S. Courts, p. 50; U.S. Courts, p. 24; U.S. Government Printing Office, p. 18; William J. Clinton Presidential Library/Smithsonian Institution, p. 93.

Cover Photo: © Corel Corporation; Supreme Court of the United States (seal)

Contents

MyReportLinks.com Books
Great Books, Great Links, Great for Research!

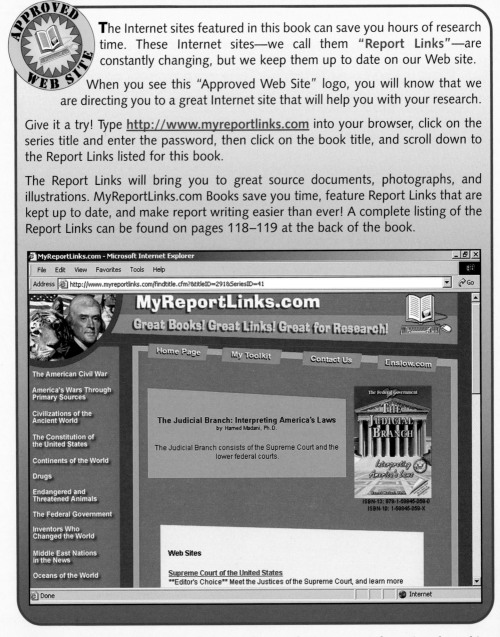

The Internet sites featured in this book can save you hours of research time. These Internet sites—we call them **"Report Links"**—are constantly changing, but we keep them up to date on our Web site.

When you see this "Approved Web Site" logo, you will know that we are directing you to a great Internet site that will help you with your research.

Give it a try! Type http://www.myreportlinks.com into your browser, click on the series title and enter the password, then click on the book title, and scroll down to the Report Links listed for this book.

The Report Links will bring you to great source documents, photographs, and illustrations. MyReportLinks.com Books save you time, feature Report Links that are kept up to date, and make report writing easier than ever! A complete listing of the Report Links can be found on pages 118–119 at the back of the book.

Please see "To Our Readers" on the copyright page for important information about this book, the MyReportLinks.com Web site, and the Report Links that back up this book.

Please enter JBA1464 if asked for a password.

BRANCHES OF THE FEDERAL GOVERNMENT

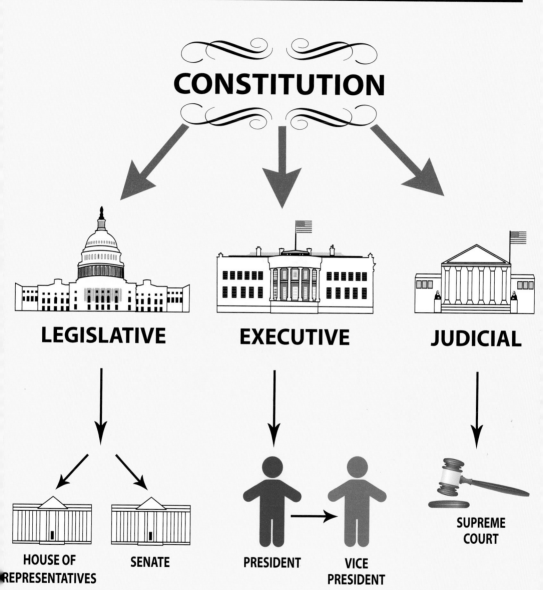

CONSTITUTION

LEGISLATIVE

EXECUTIVE

JUDICIAL

HOUSE OF REPRESENTATIVES

SENATE

PRESIDENT

VICE PRESIDENT

SUPREME COURT

Levels of the Federal Court

SUPREME COURT

- Nine Supreme Court Justices
- *Current Members:* Chief Justice John G. Roberts; Antonin Scalia; Stephen G. Breyer; Anthony Kennedy; Ruth Bader Ginsburg; David Souter; John Paul Stevens; Clarence Thomas; Samuel Alito, Jr.

FEDERAL COURTS OF APPEAL

- Thirteen circuit courts
- Hears no original cases, only appeals of district court decisions

FEDERAL DISTRICT COURT

- There are ninety-four district courts including courts in each of the fifty states as well as United States territories such as Puerto Rico.
- District courts hear almost all original federal court cases

THE UNITED STATES SUPREME COURT AND THE ELECTION OF 2000

1

The United States Supreme Court made a historic decision during the controversy over the 2000 presidential election. The decision significantly affected the outcome of that election by stopping a court-ordered recount in Florida. The Court's decision resulted in George W. Bush becoming the forty-third president of the United States.

⚖ BACKGROUND

The presidential election took place November 7, 2000. On this day, voters in all fifty states of the United States voted to elect a new president. However, the members of the electoral college, not

The entrance to the Supreme Court building, located in Washington, D.C. Many important judicial decisions have been handed down in this building.

the voters, officially decide who should be the president. The electoral college is a body of individuals chosen in fifty states and Washington, D.C., who elect the president and vice president. The members of the electoral college usually cast their votes according to who the majority of citizens in their state voted for.

To become the next president, a candidate has to have 270 out of 538 votes in the electoral college. The state of Florida had twenty-five electoral votes in 2000. To receive its twenty-five electoral votes, a presidential candidate must win the popular vote in Florida. However, the results of the Florida popular presidential election were very close. In fact, George W. Bush was not declared the president until several weeks after the day of election.

⚖ RESULTS OF FLORIDA ELECTION

In Florida, approximately 6 million people voted. George W. Bush received 2,909,135 votes. Al Gore, Jr., secured 2,907,351. Some people voted for other candidates. There was a difference of 1,784 votes or one-half of a percent between Bush and Gore. Yet there is still great uncertainty about the vote count. Florida election law allows an automatic recount of all ballots when the total vote difference is less than one percent. So, ballot recounts started immediately. However, the

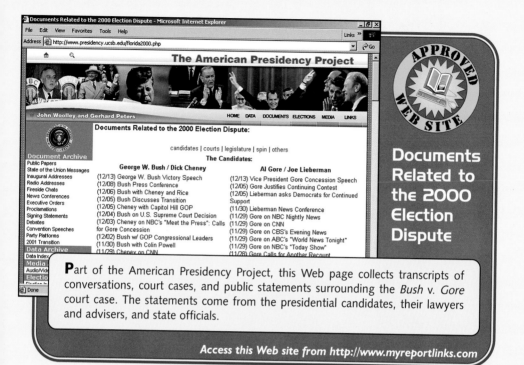

Documents Related to the 2000 Election Dispute

Part of the American Presidency Project, this Web page collects transcripts of conversations, court cases, and public statements surrounding the *Bush* v. *Gore* court case. The statements come from the presidential candidates, their lawyers and advisers, and state officials.

Access this Web site from http://www.myreportlinks.com

Florida secretary of state, Republican Katherine Harris, refused to accept any recount returns after November 14. Based on recount returns, Bush's lead was reduced from 1,784 to 930.

Some counties failed to complete their manual recounts on time. Thus, Harris certified Bush as the winner. However, Al Gore demanded continued manual recounts of ballots at least in the four largest and Democratic counties. These were Volusia, Palm Beach, Broward, and Miami-Dade counties. Gore's lawyers first argued their case before a county court trial judge. The judge dismissed Gore's lawsuit. However, the case was quickly appealed to the Florida Supreme Court.

The Florida Supreme Court ordered manual recounts of all ballots.

⚖ BUSH'S FIRST APPEAL

Bush's team of lawyers appealed the decision of the Florida Supreme Court to the United States Supreme Court. The national Court was to decide whether or not the Florida Supreme Court's ruling was constitutional. The justices first ordered a stop to the recounts. Then, the Court sent the case back to the Florida Supreme Court. The United States Supreme Court sought clarification about the Florida court's decision.

However, the Florida Supreme Court ignored the order of the United States Supreme Court. It

ordered the continued recount of all votes, especially undervotes. Undervotes were ballots discovered during the recounts, where the voting machines failed to register a vote for president. It instructed the

Former Vice President Al Gore.

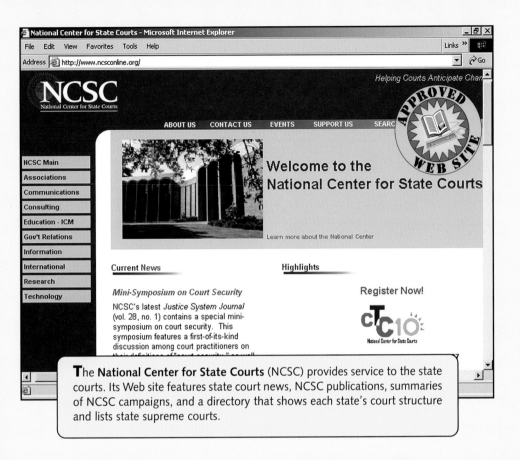

The **National Center for State Courts** (NCSC) provides service to the state courts. Its Web site features state court news, NCSC publications, summaries of NCSC campaigns, and a directory that shows each state's court structure and lists state supreme courts.

election officials that "the intent of the voter" should be the standard for deciding how to count a ballot.

⚖ BUSH'S SECOND APPEAL

The Bush lawyers immediately appealed the second decision of the Florida Supreme Court to the United States Supreme Court. By now, more than a month had passed without the world knowing who the next United States president would be. The only thing certain was that Al Gore had won the popular national vote. But the election depended on the outcome of the electoral votes in Florida. Once again, the United States Supreme Court accepted Bush's appeal.

⚖️A DIVIDED SUPREME COURT

The Court delivered its decision late in the evening of December 12, 2000. The Court stated, "The use of standardless manual recounts violates the Equal Protection and Due Process Clauses of the United States Constitution."[1] This meant that the judgment of the supreme court of Florida was reversed.

The 5–4 Supreme Court decision appeared to follow political lines. Five conservative-leaning members of the United States Supreme Court voted in the majority. Their votes certified Bush as the winner of Florida's twenty-five electoral votes. Four liberal-leaning members of the Supreme Court supported Gore's position. They argued that the United States Supreme Court should not interfere with the Florida Supreme Court's decision. Three members of the United States Supreme Court (William Rehnquist, Clarence Thomas, and Antonin Scalia), each of whom voted with the majority, argued that the recount of ballots was unconstitutional. Their reasoning was that the Florida Supreme Court's decision made a new election law. Lawmaking is the responsibility of

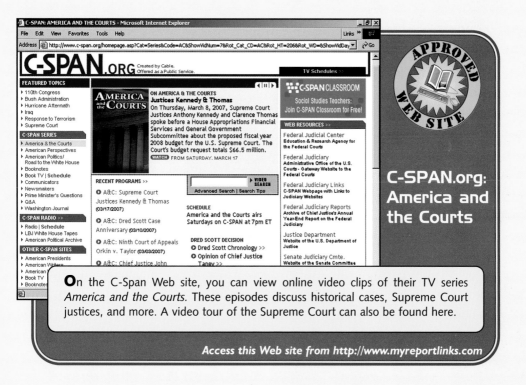

On the C-Span Web site, you can view online video clips of their TV series *America and the Courts.* These episodes discuss historical cases, Supreme Court justices, and more. A video tour of the Supreme Court can also be found here.

Access this Web site from http://www.myreportlinks.com

the state legislature, not the judiciary. Thus the United States Supreme Court ended the 2000 presidential election contest. Al Gore accepted defeat on December 13, 2000.

THE LESSON

Courts are important institutions in American society deeply involved in the life of the country and its people. Courts are responsible for resolving certain disagreements. Courts resolve disputes when people sue each other in disagreements over contracts, personal injuries, and other such matters. Courts try people who are accused of violating society's rules by committing crimes.

President George W. Bush

The *Bush* v. *Gore* Supreme Court decision shows that America's courts have another important function as well. The function has to do with affecting policy. Alexis de Tocqueville, a Frenchman who visited the United States in the early 1800s, made the following remarks with regard to this function of the courts: "There is hardly a political question in the United States which does not sooner or later turn into a judicial one."[2]

As an institution that affects policy, the courts have decided issues of great importance. They include controversies involving discrimination, the environment, and abortion, separation of church and state, and defining the rights of criminal defendants. As a result, under our system of government, individuals and groups use the opinions of the judiciary to shape the types of laws that can be passed.

ORGANIZATION AND RESPONSIBILITIES

2

The United States Constitution created three branches of federal government. These are the legislative, executive, and judicial branches. The legislative branch consists of the two houses of Congress—the House of Representatives and the Senate. The members of Congress are mainly responsible for making the laws.

The executive branch of the federal government consists of the office of the president of the United States and the executive departments. The main responsibility of the executive branch is to enforce the laws that Congress makes.

The third branch of the federal government is the judicial branch. The judicial branch consists of the Supreme Court and the other federal judges and courts. The most important role of the judicial branch is to interpret the laws that Congress has passed. This way, they can assure that the laws are constitutional and that they are being enforced without violating the rights of the American citizens.

Article III of the United States Constitution establishes the judicial branch of the federal government. The Constitution also gives Congress

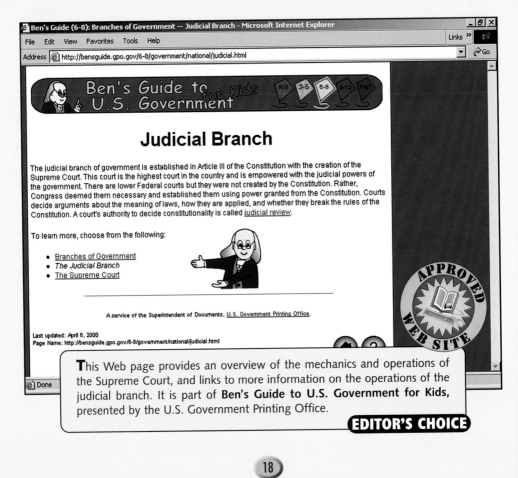

This Web page provides an overview of the mechanics and operations of the Supreme Court, and links to more information on the operations of the judicial branch. It is part of **Ben's Guide to U.S. Government for Kids,** presented by the U.S. Government Printing Office.

EDITOR'S CHOICE

authority to create lower federal courts. Congress has established two broad categories of courts, constitutional and legislative.

Article III has been used by Congress to create lower constitutional courts. Article III, Section 1 states the following, "the judicial power of the United States, shall be vested in one Supreme Court, and in such inferior courts as the Congress

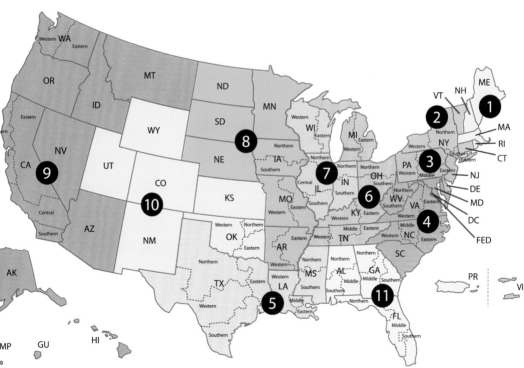

Geographic Boundaries
of United States Courts of Appeals and United States District Courts

▲ This map shows how the judicial branch serves the citizens of the United States by breaking up the federal courts into districts. Which district do you live in?

may from time to time ordain and establish." The constitutional courts include the Supreme Court of the United States, the United States Courts of Appeals, and the United States District Courts.[1]

In addition, Article I of the United States Constitution has been used by Congress to establish legislative courts. These courts handle issues that deal with lawmaking. Article I, Section 8, Clause 9 states that Congress has the power "To constitute tribunals inferior to the Supreme Court." The United States Tax Court and the United States Court of Appeals for Veterans Claims are two examples of the legislative courts. These courts interpret and apply the law to resolve disputes and to decide if certain laws are constitutional or not.

Finally, Congress has created a third type of court, those that have specialized jurisdiction. Some examples include the United States Court of Federal Claims and the United States Court of International Trade.

⚖ THE SUPREME COURT

The Supreme Court sits in Washington, D.C. It is the highest court in the United States. The Supreme Court was established in accordance with Article III, Section I of the Constitution.[2]

The president appoints members to the Supreme Court and the senators approve them by a majority vote. Supreme Court justices serve for life or until they retire. The Court originally consisted of a chief justice and five associate justices, for a total of six members. Congress changed the membership to nine in 1869, and that number has remained consistent since that time.[3] An attempt was made by President Franklin Delano Roosevelt to increase the total membership to fifteen, but Congress refused.

Among the members of the Supreme Court in 2007 there was one woman, Ruth Bader Ginsburg. President Bill Clinton appointed Justice Ginsburg in 1993. She is the second female member in the history of the Supreme Court. Sandra Day O'Connor was the first female appointed to the Supreme Court, by President Ronald Reagan in 1981. Samuel Alito replaced Justice O'Connor in 2006 after she retired.

JURISDICTION

Jurisdiction is the power of a court to hear and decide a case. There are two broad categories of jurisdiction: original and appellate. Courts of original jurisdiction hear a case for the first time. These courts are often referred to as trial courts, where witnesses testify and evidence and exhibits are introduced. Trial courts determine the facts of the case, and based on those facts, apply the existing law to reach a decision.

This image shows almost the entire front of the Supreme Court building. Construction of the building was completed in 1935.

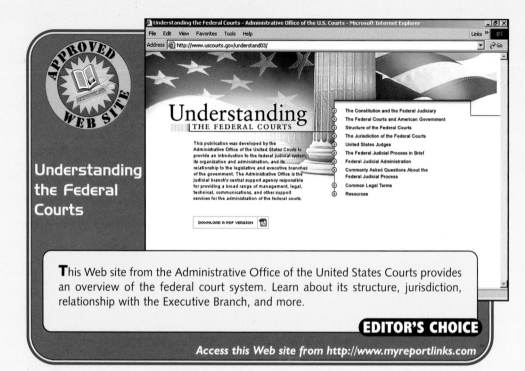

Understanding
THE FEDERAL COURTS

This publication was developed by the Administrative Office of the United States Courts to provide an introduction to the federal judicial system, its organization and administration, and its relationship to the legislative and executive branches of the government. The Administrative Office is the judicial branch's central support agency responsible for providing a broad range of management, legal, technical, communications, and other support services for the administration of the federal courts.

The Constitution and the Federal Judiciary
The Federal Courts and American Government
Structure of the Federal Courts
The Jurisdiction of the Federal Courts
United States Judges
The Federal Judicial Process in Brief
Federal Judicial Administration
Commonly Asked Questions About the Federal Judicial Process
Common Legal Terms
Resources

DOWNLOAD A PDF VERSION

Understanding the Federal Courts

This Web site from the Administrative Office of the United States Courts provides an overview of the federal court system. Learn about its structure, jurisdiction, relationship with the Executive Branch, and more.

EDITOR'S CHOICE

Access this Web site from http://www.myreportlinks.com

If the decision of a trial court is appealed, an appellate court reviews the case. Appellate courts determine whether the trial court correctly applied the law and followed established legal procedures. An appellate court may let stand the trial court's decision, overturn the trial court's verdict, or send the case back to the trial court for another hearing.

⚖ ORIGINAL JURISDICTION OF THE SUPREME COURT

The Supreme Court is the only federal court with both original and appellate jurisdiction. The original jurisdiction of the Supreme Court is limited.

It resolves disputes between two or more states, disputes involving ambassadors and other diplomats, and disputes against the federal government. It also resolves disputes between a state against a citizen of another state or country if initiated by a state of the United States.

The Court rarely exercises its original jurisdiction, and Congress has allowed lower federal courts to also try these controversies. The Supreme Court is the only court that can hear disputes between two or more states. In 1998, for example, it heard a dispute between New York and New Jersey over ownership of Ellis Island.

⚖ APPELLATE JURISDICTION OF THE SUPREME COURT

The Supreme Court's most important jurisdiction is appellate. With regard to the appellate jurisdiction of the Supreme Court, Article III, Section 2 of the Constitution states, "In all the other Cases before mentioned, the Supreme Court shall have appellate Jurisdiction. . . ." The Supreme Court exercises discretion when considering whether to accept an appeal.[4] In other words, citizens cannot appeal their cases as a matter of right. The Supreme Court can hear cases appealed from both lower federal courts and state supreme courts. But, any appeal of a state court decision must

One of the duties of the Supreme Court is to resolve disputes between states. One such example was a conflict between New York and New Jersey over the jurisdiction of Ellis Island (shown here).

involve an issue of federal law. Cases accepted by the Supreme Court involve important questions about the Constitution or federal law.

⚖ SUPREME COURT'S APPELLATE PROCEDURES

Approximately seventy-five hundred cases are appealed to the Supreme Court each year. The Supreme Court usually accepts only eighty to one hundred of these cases. In 2006, they only accepted sixty-eight. Cases can be brought to the court by appeal or by *writ of certiorari*. The Court reviews cases on appeal from federal courts or state supreme courts such as when a federal appeals court invalidates a state law, or when a state court strikes down a federal law. Therefore, a party who wishes for the Court to hear an appeal must file a writ of certiorari—informally called a "Cert Petition." Certiorari is a Latin phrase meaning "to be made certain in regard to." It is a document filed by a party with the Supreme Court asking the Court to review the decision of a lower court.

⚖ WRITTEN BRIEFS

If the Supreme Court accepts a case, the case is usually scheduled for briefing and argument. Four of the nine justices of the Supreme Court must vote to accept a petition for certiorari. This is informally called the "Rule of Four." Following the acceptance of a cert petition, parties to a case submit written briefs. These are detailed legal arguments of a case. Another type of brief filed with the court is an *amicus curiae* brief, also known as a "friend of the court" brief. Amicus briefs are usually filed by organizations or government agencies that are not a party to the case. Yet these organizations believe that the Court's decision may affect their interest. For example, in the case of *Harris* v. *Forklift System* (1993), the Supreme Court unanimously ruled that Teresa

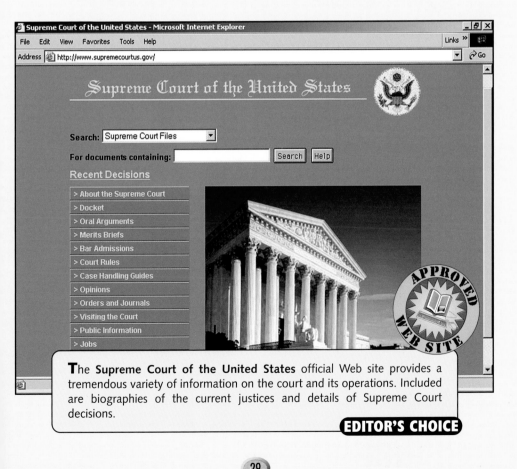

The **Supreme Court of the United States** official Web site provides a tremendous variety of information on the court and its operations. Included are biographies of the current justices and details of Supreme Court decisions.

EDITOR'S CHOICE

Harris was subjected to sexual harassment. In her support, over forty different groups and government agencies filed amicus curiae briefs. Among them were the Equal Employment Opportunity Commission, Center for Women's Policy Studies, Trial Lawyers for Public Justice, American Civil Liberties Union, and California Women Lawyers.

⚖ ORAL ARGUMENT

After receiving written briefs from both sides, an oral argument may be, but is not always held. The parties appealing to the Supreme Court must request oral argument. Oral arguments take place in public in the Supreme Court chamber. Lawyers from both sides appear before the nine justices. The lawyers summarize their positions before the Court. Justices may question the lawyers during the course of their presentations. Attorneys from each side are given one hour to present their oral arguments.

⚖ CONFERENCE AND DECISION

After the justices study all briefs, lower court rulings, and other research, they meet together behind closed doors to discuss each case. They share their opinions and debate the issues. Eventually, the Court comes to a conclusion and announces its decision. When the Court announces its decision, each individual justice's opinion is revealed. A unanimous decision (9–0) indicates that all justices were in total agreement. A majority opinion may also be prepared, and justices whose point of view did not prevail release a dissenting or minority opinion. A justice who agrees with the majority, but for different reasons, sometimes presents a concurring opinion. These opinions are later collected and published in the *United States Reports,* the official record of the Court's work.

⚖ POWER OF JUDICIAL REVIEW

The most important responsibility of the Supreme Court is the power of judicial review. It is the power of the Court to reject a state or national law as unconstitutional. Any court can exercise judicial review, but all lower court decisions and state court decisions ruling on federal law are subject to review by the Supreme Court. There is no mention of the power of judicial review in the Constitution. Chief Justice John Marshall interpreted the Constitution to support judicial review in the case of *Marbury* v. *Madison* (1803). Justice Marshall declared that it is the duty of the judicial branch "to say what the law is." This decision, and this statement, established the concept of judicial review.

This is one of the many statues decorating the exterior of the Supreme Court building. Architect Cass Gilbert was mainly responsible for the building's structure.

⚖ COURTS OF APPEALS

There are thirteen courts of appeals throughout the United States. They are often referred to as circuit courts. That is because early in the nation's history, the judges visited each of the courts, traveling by horseback and riding the "circuit." Twelve of these courts have jurisdiction over cases from certain geographic areas. For example, the Fifth Circuit Court of Appeals has jurisdiction over Texas, Mississippi, and Louisiana. The D.C. Circuit has jurisdiction over Washington, D.C., but also hears a number of cases involving federal agencies, boards, and commissions. Examples include cases involving the Environmental Protection

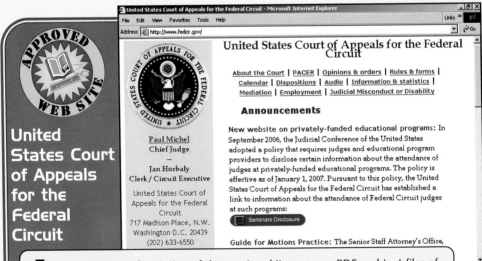

APPROVED WEB SITE

United States Court of Appeals for the Federal Circuit

United States Court of Appeals for the Federal Circuit - Microsoft Internet Explorer

File   Edit   View   Favorites   Tools   Help

Address http://www.fedcir.gov/

United States Court of Appeals for the Federal Circuit

About the Court | PACER | Opinions & orders | Rules & forms | Calendar | Dispositions | Audio | Information & statistics | Mediation | Employment | Judicial Misconduct or Disability

Announcements

Paul Michel
Chief Judge
—
Jan Horbaly
Clerk / Circuit Executive

United States Court of Appeals for the Federal Circuit
717 Madison Place, N.W.
Washington D.C. 20439
(202) 633-6550

New website on privately-funded educational programs: In September 2006, the Judicial Conference of the United States adopted a policy that requires judges and educational program providers to disclose certain information about the attendance of judges at privately-funded educational programs. The policy is effective as of January 1, 2007. Pursuant to this policy, the United States Court of Appeals for the Federal Circuit has established a link to information about the attendance of Federal Circuit judges at such programs:

Seminars Disclosure

Guide for Motions Practice: The Senior Staff Attorney's Office,

This site contains a description of the court and its purpose, PDF and text files of Opinions and Orders dating back to October 2004, biographies of current judges, a frequently asked questions section (FAQ), and MP3 audio of recent oral arguments.

Access this Web site from http://www.myreportlinks.com

Agency, the National Labor Relations Board, and the Federal Communications Commission.

⚖ U.S. COURT OF APPEALS FOR THE FEDERAL CIRCUIT

In 1982, Congress created the United States Court of Appeals for the Federal Circuit, also simply known as the Federal Circuit. It combines the functions of the United States Court of Customs and Patent Appeals and the United States Court of Claims.

Unlike the other twelve courts of appeals, the Federal Circuit has national jurisdiction. It is located in Washington, D.C. It accepts appeals in patent, trademark, and copyright cases. Patent is the exclusive right given to an inventor for a fixed period to prevent others from making, using, selling, or importing the claimed invention. A trademark is a special name, word, or symbol that can only be used for the thing made by that business. A copyright is a law that gives the creator of a document such as musical piece the right to its creation and distribution.[5] The U.S. Court of Appeals for the Federal Circuit also accepts cases from the United States Court of Federal Claims, the United States Court of Veterans Appeals, the International Trade Commission, the Merit Systems Protection Board, and from the United States Court of International Trade.

⚖ JURISDICTION OF COURTS OF APPEALS

Courts of appeals have appellate jurisdiction. The losing party in a decision by a federal trial court is entitled to appeal the decision to a federal court of appeals. In a civil case, either side may appeal the decision of a court. In a criminal case, the defendant may appeal a guilty decision of a court. A prosecutor can only appeal if he or she disagrees with a judge's

▲ Every case decided by the Supreme Court is highly scrutinized. The decisions and opinions of the justices are required reading for many lawyers.

sentence. A defendant who files an appeal must show that the trial court did not correctly apply the law to the case or did not follow established legal procedures.

The court of appeals makes its decision based on the trial record. The trial record is the facts of the case that have been written down. The record is established by the trial court and usually includes witness testimony and evidence. Appellate courts do not receive additional evidence or hear from live witnesses.

APPELLATE PROCEDURES

In the federal system, a panel of three judges usually decides an appeal. An appeal is made in writing, in a document called a written brief. In the brief, the appealing party tries to convince the court that the trial court made an error. On the other hand, the party defending against the appeal tries to show why the trial court decision was correct. Ultimately, the appellate court will decide to either uphold or reverse the decision of the trial court. The court of appeals decision is final, unless the parties ask the United States Supreme Court to review the case. In some cases, the decision may be reviewed by all the judges of the court of appeals. This type of review is called *en banc* review, and is reserved for very special cases.

⚖ COURT OF APPEALS JUDGES

Each court of appeals consists of six or more judges; the total number depends on the caseload of the court. For example, the First Circuit Court of Appeals has six judges, while the Ninth Circuit Court of Appeals has twenty-eight judges because the Ninth Circuit is presented with more cases. These judges are appointed by the president and confirmed by a majority vote of the Senate. Federal appellate judges are appointed for life. The judge who has served the longest and who

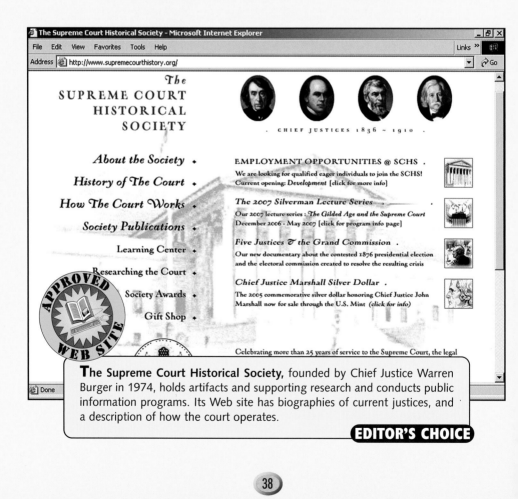

The Supreme Court Historical Society, founded by Chief Justice Warren Burger in 1974, holds artifacts and supporting research and conducts public information programs. Its Web site has biographies of current justices, and a description of how the court operates.

EDITOR'S CHOICE

is under sixty-five years old is designated as the chief judge. The chief judge serves for a maximum term of seven years. There are approximately 167 judges on the 12 regional courts of appeals. The Federal Circuit has twelve judges. Like other judges of courts of appeals, the judges of the Federal Circuit are appointed by the president and confirmed by the Senate. They also serve for life.

⚖ DISTRICT COURTS

The United States District Courts are federal trial courts. Both civil and criminal cases are filed in the district courts. There are ninety-four federal districts. Ninety of these are located in the fifty states and Washington, D.C. Each state has at least one federal district court and as many as four, based on its population. For example, Texas has four district courts: the Northern District in Dallas, the Southern District in Houston, the Eastern District in Tyler, and the Western District in San Antonio. Each district court has between two and twenty-eight judges. The remaining four district courts are located in the Commonwealth of Puerto Rico, the territories of Guam, the United States Virgin Islands, and the Northern Mariana Islands. The last three courts are also known as territorial courts. They function as both state and local courts as well as federal courts. Their judges are

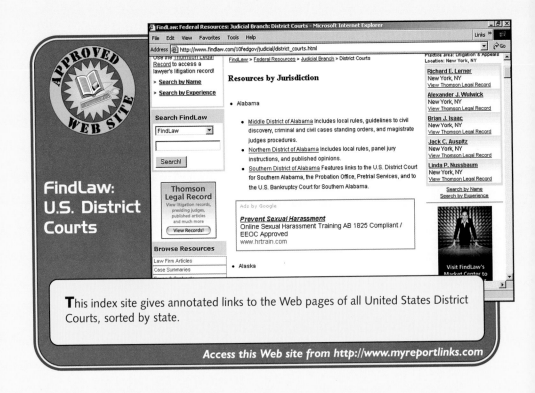

FindLaw:
U.S. District
Courts

This index site gives annotated links to the Web pages of all United States District Courts, sorted by state.

Access this Web site from http://www.myreportlinks.com

appointed by the president and confirmed by the Senate. They serve for a term of ten years.

JURISDICTION OF DISTRICT COURTS

The jurisdiction of the district courts is defined in Article III, Section 2 of the Constitution. There are two main types of jurisdictions: federal question jurisdiction and diversity jurisdiction.

FEDERAL QUESTION JURISDICTION

Federal district courts may hear cases that involve issues dealing with the U.S. Constitution and federal laws. The source of federal question jurisdiction can be found in Article III of the

Constitution. Article III states that the "judicial power shall extend to all cases, in law and equity, arising under this Constitution, the laws of the United States, and Treaties made, or which shall be made, under their Authority."

For example, a dispute between a property owner and a tenant over rent would normally not be a federal question. This is because the relationships between property owners and tenants usually arise under state law rather than federal law. However, the tenant could argue that she was being discriminated against based on her race. A federal law, the Fair Housing Act, protects the rights of tenants against racial discrimination. If the tenant claims that the property owner is violating the Fair Housing Act, she could bring her case to federal court because it raises a federal question.

⚖ DIVERSITY JURISDICTION

Federal law also authorizes federal courts to hear cases where parties in a dispute are citizens of different states. This is known as diversity jurisdiction, because the parties have different state citizenships. The federal law governing diversity jurisdiction states that a case must have an "amount-in-controversy" exceeding seventy-five thousand dollars before a federal court can hear a case. Federal question jurisdiction, on the other hand, does not have any amount-in-controversy requirement.

LEGISLATIVE COURTS

The Supreme Court has identified three situations in which Congress may create legislative courts. First, Congress may create legislative courts in United States territories, such as Guam or Puerto Rico. These are called territorial courts. Second, Congress may create legislative courts to hear military cases. The United States Court of Military Appeals is such a court. Finally, Congress may

U.S. Court of Appeals for the Armed Forces - Microsoft Internet Explorer

File   Edit   View   Favorites   Tools   Help   Links »

Address http://www.armfor.uscourts.gov/index.html   Go

U.S. COURT OF APPEALS
FOR THE ARMED FORCES

Search Site

◆ Establishment
  -- Court Brochure (pdf *)
◆ Appellate Review
◆ Practice & Procedure
◆ Judges
      Clerkships
    & Digest
    ...l
    ...ispositions
    ...orts

◆ Scheduled Hearings
  (Includes Audio Files)
◆ Code Committee
◆ Court Rules
◆ Bar
◆ Judicial Conference
◆ Clerk's Office
  -- E-Filing
◆ Library
◆ Other Web Sites

Geared primarily to professionals, the **U.S. Court of Appeals for the Armed Forces** Web site also provides a brochure with a court overview, history, details of its operation, and information on its justices. Other site materials include a daily journal of court actions, and opinions from recent years.

create legislative courts to hear cases involving public rights. One example of such a court is the United States Tax Court.[6]

⚖️ UNITED STATES COURT OF MILITARY APPEALS

Congress created the United States Court of Military Appeals in 1951. At that time, Congress also enacted the Uniform Code of Military Justice, which established a military judicial system. This system was designed to balance the need to maintain discipline in the armed forces with the need to give members of the military services who are accused of crimes rights like those of accused persons in the civilian community. The court was renamed as the Court of Appeals for the Armed Forces in 1994.

The court's jurisdiction is worldwide but encompasses only questions of law arising from trials by court-martial in the United States Army, Navy, Air Force, Marine Corps, and Coast Guard. These include cases where a death sentence is imposed, where a case is certified for review by the judge advocate general of the accused's service, or where the accused who faces a severe sentence petitions and shows good cause for further review. Such cases are subject to further review by the Supreme Court of the United States. The Supreme Court also has jurisdiction to review

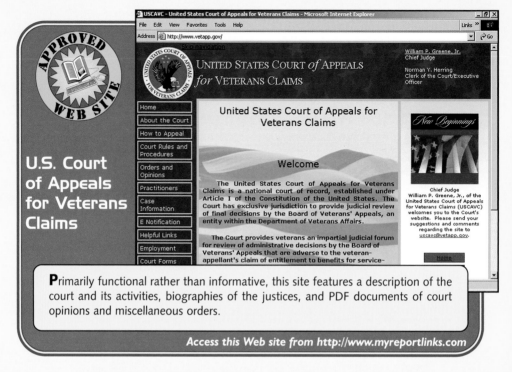

USCAVC - United States Court of Appeals for Veterans Claims - Microsoft Internet Explorer

File   Edit   View   Favorites   Tools   Help   Links »

Address http://www.vetapp.gov/   ▼ ⌀ Go

Skip navigation

UNITED STATES COURT *of* APPEALS
for VETERANS CLAIMS

William P. Greene, Jr.
Chief Judge

Norman Y. Herring
Clerk of the Court/Executive
Officer

Home
About the Court
How to Appeal
Court Rules and Procedures
Orders and Opinions
Practitioners
Case Information
E Notification
Helpful Links
Employment
Court Forms

United States Court of Appeals for
Veterans Claims

New Beginnings

Welcome

The United States Court of Appeals for Veterans Claims is a national court of record, established under Article I of the Constitution of the United States. The Court has exclusive jurisdiction to provide judicial review of final decisions by the Board of Veterans' Appeals, an entity within the Department of Veterans Affairs.

The Court provides veterans an impartial judicial forum for review of administrative decisions by the Board of Veterans' Appeals that are adverse to the veteran-appellant's claim of entitlement to benefits for service-

Chief Judge
William P. Greene, Jr., of the
United States Court of Appeals
for Veterans Claims (USCAVC)
welcomes you to the Court's
website. Please send your
suggestions and comments
regarding the site to
uscavc@vetapp.gov.

Home

U.S. Court
of Appeals
for Veterans
Claims

Primarily functional rather than informative, this site features a description of the court and its activities, biographies of the justices, and PDF documents of court opinions and miscellaneous orders.

Access this Web site from http://www.myreportlinks.com

decisions of the military appellate courts if some-
one appeals a ruling handed down by the military
judge during a court-martial.

The five judges of the Court of Military Appeals
are civilians (citizens who are not serving in the
Armed Forces) appointed for fifteen-year terms by
the president on the advice and consent of the
Senate. The chief judge serves for five years and is
succeeded by the next senior judge on the court.
This court is located in Washington, D.C.

⚖ UNITED STATES COURT OF VETERANS APPEALS

Congress created the United States Court of Veterans Appeals in 1988 to review the decisions of the

Board of Veterans' Appeals. Such cases include disputes over all types of veterans and survivors' benefits, mainly disability benefits, and also loan eligibility and educational benefits. In the year which ended June 30, 1992, the United States Court of Veterans Appeals reviewed 1,931 cases and terminated 1,897. Its decisions are subject to limited review by the United States Court of Appeals for the Federal Circuit.

The court has seven judgeships. The judges of the court are appointed by the president on the advice and consent of the Senate. The court is

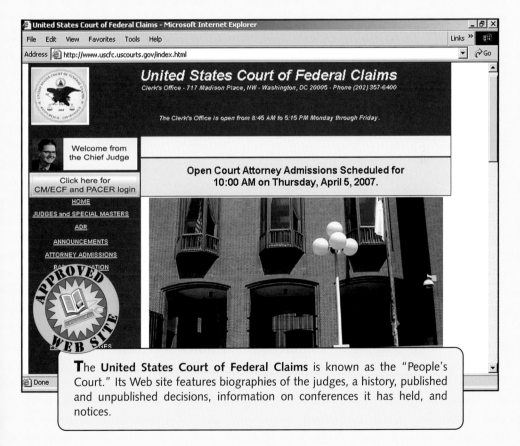

The **United States Court of Federal Claims** is known as the "People's Court." Its Web site features biographies of the judges, a history, published and unpublished decisions, information on conferences it has held, and notices.

based in Washington, D.C., but as a national court, it may sit anywhere in the United States.

⚖ UNITED STATES COURT OF FEDERAL CLAIMS

The United States Court of Federal Claims, formerly the U.S. Claims Court, was established in 1982. It succeeded the trial division of the Court of Claims, which had been in existence since 1855. The U.S. Court of Federal Claims has nationwide jurisdiction over a variety of cases. Some examples are:

⚖ Disputes over tax refunds

⚖ Federal taking of private property for public use

⚖ Constitutional and statutory rights of military personnel and their dependents

⚖ Back-pay demands from civil servants claiming unjust dismissal

⚖ Persons injured by childhood vaccines

⚖ Federal government contractors suing for breach of contract

However, the federal district courts have sole discretion over tort claims (a civil wrong or breach of duty) and also have jurisdiction over tax refunds. The United States Court of Federal Claims hears appeals of decisions of the Indian Claims Commission. In addition, the court has the authority to review certain cases involving federal government contractor disputes. Either house of Congress may refer to the chief judge a claim for which there is no legal remedy. In this case the lawmakers will seek advice on whether there is an equitable basis which Congress itself should compensate the claimant. Reviews of decisions in the U.S. Court of Federal Claims are done by the United States Court of Appeals for the Federal Circuit.

The sixteen judges of the United States Claims Court are appointed for terms of fifteen years by the president on the advice and consent of the Senate. The court's headquarters is in Washington, D.C., but cases are heard at other locations convenient to the parties involved.

⚖ UNITED STATES TAX COURT

Established by Congress in 1924 under Article I of the Constitution, the United States Tax Court decides controversies between taxpayers and the Internal Revenue Service involving underpayment of federal income, gift, and estate taxes. Its decisions may be appealed to the federal courts of appeals and are subject to the review of the United States Supreme Court on writs of certiorari.

The president appoints the nineteen tax court judges for terms of fifteen years. The judges of the court elect one member among themselves to serve a two-year term as chief judge. The chief

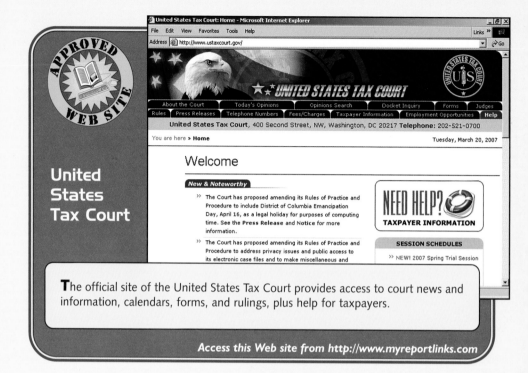

United States Tax Court: Home - Microsoft Internet Explorer

File   Edit   View   Favorites   Tools   Help   Links »

Address http://www.ustaxcourt.gov/   Go

★·★ UNITED STATES TAX COURT

About the Court | Today's Opinions | Opinions Search | Docket Inquiry | Forms | Judges
Rules | Press Releases | Telephone Numbers | Fees/Charges | Taxpayer Information | Employment Opportunities | Help

United States Tax Court, 400 Second Street, NW, Washington, DC 20217 Telephone: 202-521-0700

You are here > Home   Tuesday, March 20, 2007

Welcome

New & Noteworthy

» The Court has proposed amending its Rules of Practice and Procedure to include District of Columbia Emancipation Day, April 16, as a legal holiday for purposes of computing time. See the **Press Release** and **Notice** for more information.

» The Court has proposed amending its Rules of Practice and Procedure to address privacy issues and public access to its electronic case files and to make miscellaneous and

NEED HELP?
TAXPAYER INFORMATION

SESSION SCHEDULES
» NEW! 2007 Spring Trial Session

United States Tax Court

The official site of the United States Tax Court provides access to court news and information, calendars, forms, and rulings, plus help for taxpayers.

Access this Web site from http://www.myreportlinks.com

judge has responsibility for overall administration of the court in addition to a caseload. Retired judges may be recalled by the chief judge for service in the court. In addition, there are currently seventeen authorized special trial judges appointed by the chief judge, who serve under rules and regulations promulgated by the court.

The Tax Court hears cases in approximately eighty cities. Its main offices are located in Washington, D.C.

⚖ SPECIALIZED COURTS

Finally, Congress has created a number of federal courts that have specialized jurisdiction. One

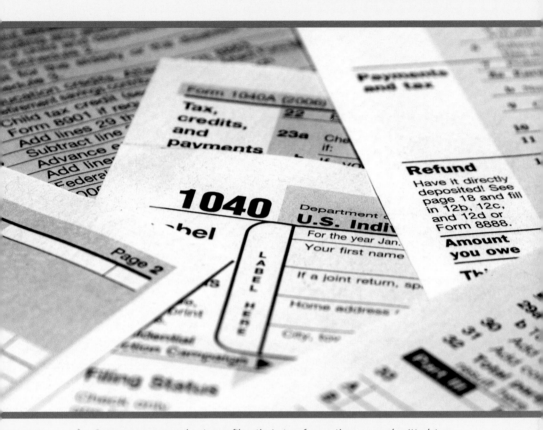

△ *Once a person or business files their tax forms they are submitted to the Internal Revenue Service. Sometimes there are disputes between those filing and the IRS. The U.S. Tax Court was created to resolve those disputes.*

example is the United States Court of Federal Claims, which has already been discussed. Another is the Court of International Trade.

⚖ COURT OF INTERNATIONAL TRADE

Congress established the Court of International Trade in 1980. It used to be called the United States Customs Court. This court tries cases involving international trade and customs duties.

United
States
Court of
International
Trade

Website of the United States Court of International Trade - Microsoft Internet Explorer

File   Edit   View   Favorites   Tools   Help

Links »

Address http://www.cit.uscourts.gov/

Go

Important Notices:

Notice of Amendments to the Court's Rules and
Forms that will become effective Jan. 1 2007.

Open a Case in CM/ECF starting October 11, 2006

Welcome to the Website of the

United States Court of International Trade

◈ Search the Court's Website
◈ Weekly Court Calendar
◈ About the Court

This court is responsible for international trade legislation. So, its Web site is geared to attorneys, including slip (unpublished) opinions from 1999 to present in PDF format. However, the "About" section contains easy-to-understand information on the court's history and practices.

Access this Web site from http://www.myreportlinks.com

Most of its cases concern classification and appraisal of imported goods, customs duties, and unfair practices by trading partners. Appeals from this court are heard by the United States Court of Appeals for Federal Circuit.

The court has nine judges. The president appoints these judges for life on the advice and consent of the Senate. The court is located in New York.

HISTORY OF THE JUDICIARY

3

1n this chapter, we will examine specific events and personalities that have helped shape the history and direction of the judiciary. We begin with the first act of Congress, which established the federal judiciary and end with the current Supreme Court under the leadership of the newly appointed Chief Justice John Roberts.

⚖ THE JUDICIARY ACT OF 1789

The Judiciary Act of 1789 was a law passed by Congress in its first session. This law organized the United States federal judiciary. Although altered throughout the years by Congress, the basic structure of the judiciary remains largely intact. The Judiciary Act created two lower levels of federal courts: the district courts and the circuit, or appellate, courts. Another clause of the Judiciary Act set the number of Supreme Court justices at six, consisting of a Chief Justice and five associate justices. However, ninety years later Congress increased the size of the Supreme Court. The Judiciary Act of 1869 increased the number of Supreme Court justices to the current number of nine. The same act gave the Supreme Court original jurisdiction over civil disputes between two or more states, or between a state and the United States, as well as all suits brought against diplomats.

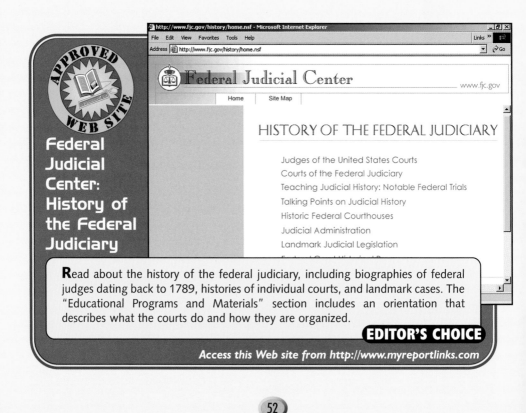

Federal Judicial Center: History of the Federal Judiciary

http://www.fjc.gov/history/home.nsf - Microsoft Internet Explorer

File   Edit   View   Favorites   Tools   Help

Address http://www.fjc.gov/history/home.nsf

Federal Judicial Center   www.fjc.gov

Home   Site Map

HISTORY OF THE FEDERAL JUDICIARY

Judges of the United States Courts
Courts of the Federal Judiciary
Teaching Judicial History: Notable Federal Trials
Talking Points on Judicial History
Historic Federal Courthouses
Judicial Administration
Landmark Judicial Legislation

Read about the history of the federal judiciary, including biographies of federal judges dating back to 1789, histories of individual courts, and landmark cases. The "Educational Programs and Materials" section includes an orientation that describes what the courts do and how they are organized.

EDITOR'S CHOICE

Access this Web site from http://www.myreportlinks.com

In addition, the 1869 Judiciary Act divided the United States into thirteen districts. The act further divided the thirteen districts into three courts of appeals or circuit courts. They were referred to as the eastern, middle, and the southern circuit. The judges of these circuits were made up of any two members of the Supreme Court and the district court judge of such districts. They traveled to each district to hear cases twice a year. Thus, the name circuit courts of appeals. Faced with a sharp increase in the number of federal lawsuits, Congress in 1869 created a judgeship for each of the nine circuits in place at that time.[1]

⚖ JOHN MARSHALL AND THE JUDICIARY

One of the famous past members of the federal judiciary is John Marshall. He was the fourth Chief Justice of the Supreme Court. John Marshall served as President John Adams's secretary of state before being nominated as the Chief Justice. The Senate confirmed Justice Marshall in 1801. He remained the head of the Supreme Court for thirty-four years, until he died in 1835. Justice Marshall remains the longest-serving Chief Justice in Supreme Court history.

Justice Marshall played a significant role in the development of the American judiciary. He improved and strengthened the image and power of the judiciary. Prior to Justice Marshall, the

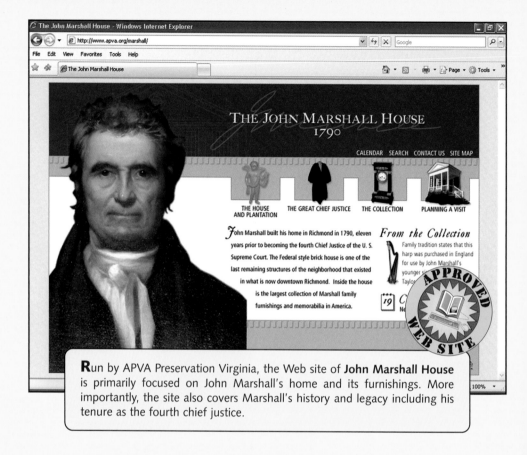

The John Marshall House - Windows Internet Explorer

http://www.apva.org/marshall/

File   Edit   View   Favorites   Tools   Help

The John Marshall House

Page ▾   Tools ▾

THE JOHN MARSHALL HOUSE
1790

CALENDAR   SEARCH   CONTACT US   SITE MAP

THE HOUSE
AND PLANTATION   THE GREAT CHIEF JUSTICE   THE COLLECTION   PLANNING A VISIT

*J*ohn Marshall built his home in Richmond in 1790, eleven
years prior to becoming the fourth Chief Justice of the U. S.
Supreme Court. The Federal style brick house is one of the
last remaining structures of the neighborhood that existed
in what is now downtown Richmond. Inside the house
is the largest collection of Marshall family
furnishings and memorabilia in America.

From the Collection

Family tradition states that this
harp was purchased in England
for use by John Marshall's
younger
Taylo

APPROVED
WEB SITE

Run by APVA Preservation Virginia, the Web site of **John Marshall House**
is primarily focused on John Marshall's home and its furnishings. More
importantly, the site also covers Marshall's history and legacy including his
tenure as the fourth chief justice.

members of the Supreme Court were not sure they
had the power to consider the constitutionality of
laws passed by Congress. Marshall argued that the
courts were entitled to do so. Thus, John Marshall
is credited with making the judiciary an important
and influential branch of the federal government.

Marshall is also remembered for decisions
made while he was on the Court. These decisions
helped the federal government gain the respect of
the United States citizens. Using *Marbury* v. *Madison* (1803), Marshall declared the power of the

Supreme Court to invalidate an act of Congress if the act was in conflict with the Constitution. *Marbury* v. *Madison* also established the concept of judicial review. In another case, *McCulloch* v. *Maryland* (1819), Marshall ruled that Congress acted constitutionally when it established a national bank. The Court held that states could not tax federal institutions. Justice Marshall further expanded the meaning of commerce and asserted Congress's power over commerce in the case of *Gibbons* v. *Ogden* (1824). In the last two cases, the decisions of the Supreme Court gave the judiciary the power to set aside state laws found to be in conflict with the Constitution.

⚖ THE IMPEACHMENT OF SAMUEL CHASE

Another event that contributed to the development of the judiciary is the impeachment of Samuel Chase. Impeachment is a process of bringing charges against certain high government officials for misconduct while in office. Impeachment is discussed in detail under Article I, Sections 2 and 3, and Article II, Section 4. The House of Representatives has the power to bring charges against an official with a majority vote. Once impeached, the official is tried by the Senate. Conviction requires the vote of two thirds of the members of the Senate, or sixty-seven senators if all one hundred members are present on the floor of the Senate. Conviction would result in removal from office.[2]

Congress exercised its impeachment power against Samuel Chase, a member of the Supreme Court, for the first and only time in 1805. His impeachment was politically motivated. President George Washington appointed Samuel Chase to the Supreme Court in 1796. He belonged to the Federalist Party, the party of George Washington. The Federalist Party favored a strong national government. When Samuel Chase expressed Federalist opinions in the Court, President Thomas Jefferson did not like it. He was an Anti-Federalist, or opponent of the Federalist Party.

The impeachment proceedings were an unsuccessful attempt on the part of Jefferson's administration to rid itself of the Federalist judges. The president encouraged Congress to impeach Samuel Chase.

◁ Samuel Chase was a Supreme Court justice appointed by President George Washington. He was later impeached for political reasons, but was not removed from the Court.

President Jefferson was confident of his decision. A majority of the members of both chambers of Congress belonged to Jefferson's party, the Democratic-Republican Party.

After a majority vote, the House of Representatives brought several charges against Samuel Chase in March 1804. Among them, Chase was accused of not giving the defendant, John Fries, a fair trial while Chase was a district court judge. John Fries was the leader of a group whose members refused to pay their property taxes. Fries was tried for subversion (undermining the government) before Samuel Chase's court and was sentenced to be hanged. However, then-President John Adams pardoned Fries.

Due to a lack of the required two-thirds vote on the floor of the Senate, Samuel Chase was acquitted. He stayed on the job as a member of the Supreme Court until he died in 1811. His acquittal has ensured an independent judiciary as one of the three branches of federal government.[3]

CHIEF JUSTICE ROGER B. TANEY AND THE CIVIL WAR

President Andrew Jackson appointed Roger B. Taney to succeed John Marshall as the fifth chief justice of the Supreme Court. Taney was a member of Jackson's Cabinet prior to becoming the new chief justice. Taney had served as the

Roger Taney was the fifth chief justice of the United States, succeeding John Marshall.

attorney general and acting secretary of treasury. As chief justice, he is best remembered as the author of the majority opinion in *Dred Scott* v. *Sandford* in 1857. Dred Scott was a runaway slave who had lived in the free state of Illinois and the free territory of Wisconsin. He moved to the slave state of Missouri, where his former master reclaimed him. He appealed to the Supreme Court in hopes of gaining his freedom.[4]

Taney, who wrote the majority opinion in the case, held that slaves were not citizens and could not sue in the federal court. He further ruled that Congress could not forbid slavery in the territories of the United States. Slaves are property according to the

Dred Scott was an escaped slave who sought to maintain his freedom after his former master reclaimed him.

United States Constitution, wrote Taney, and
the due process clause of the Fifth Amendment
protects property. Thus, the case declared the
Missouri Compromise Act of 1820 unconstitutional. The Missouri Compromise had prohibited
slavery for all new states north of 36 degrees and
30 minutes latitude.

The *Dred Scott* decision was widely condemned.
Justice Taney remained a controversial figure after
his death. Some historians blamed his decision for
making the Civil War inevitable. The Civil War
began four years after the *Dred Scott* decision. It
was finally overturned with the adoption of the
Thirteenth Amendment in 1865. This amendment
abolished slavery.

THE SUPREME COURT AFTER THE CIVIL WAR

Until the Civil War, the two main questions
before the Supreme Court were about the
strength and authority of the federal government
and slavery. These two issues of building a new
nation in America were resolved by strengthen-
ing the federal government. After the Civil War,
the Court focused its attention on government
regulation of the economy. All levels of government started passing laws to regulate, or
manage, business activities. Among these regulations were laws against monopolies, regulations

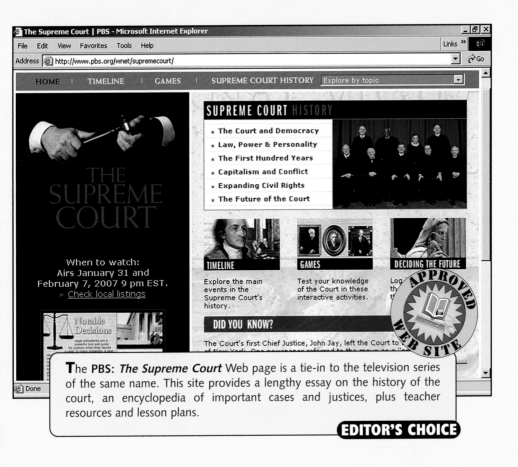

The Supreme Court | PBS - Microsoft Internet Explorer

File   Edit   View   Favorites   Tools   Help   Links »

Address http://www.pbs.org/wnet/supremecourt/   Go

HOME | TIMELINE | GAMES | SUPREME COURT HISTORY   Explore by topic

THE SUPREME COURT

When to watch:
Airs January 31 and
February 7, 2007 9 pm EST.
► Check local listings

Notable
Decisions

SUPREME COURT HISTORY

■ The Court and Democracy
■ Law, Power & Personality
■ The First Hundred Years
■ Capitalism and Conflict
■ Expanding Civil Rights
■ The Future of the Court

TIMELINE
Explore the main events in the Supreme Court's history.

GAMES
Test your knowledge of the Court in these interactive activities.

DECIDING THE FUTURE

DID YOU KNOW?
The Court's first Chief Justice, John Jay, left the Court to

Done

The **PBS:** *The Supreme Court* Web page is a tie-in to the television series of the same name. This site provides a lengthy essay on the history of the court, an encyclopedia of important cases and justices, plus teacher resources and lesson plans.

EDITOR'S CHOICE

APPROVED WEB SITE

of railroad practices, and employment conditions. Most of the above regulations were challenged in the courts.[5]

Although the Supreme Court upheld many government policies regulating business during this period, it slowly became less friendly toward those regulatory policies. The Court attempted to limit government power to control business activities and to regulate the economy. In addition, the Court showed little interest in protecting civil liberties. For example, in *Plessy* v. *Ferguson,* the Court

The Court's decision in Plessy v. Ferguson *led to legal segregation. This photo is of the drinking fountain for African Americans outside of the courthouse in Halifax, North Carolina.*

upheld the racial segregation of public facilities if they were "separate but equal."

⚖ THE ROOSEVELT YEARS

Franklin Delano Roosevelt was elected president during the Great Depression, a severe economic crisis that began in 1929. President Roosevelt introduced a group of federally funded programs known as the New Deal to lift the country out of the Great Depression. The conservative-dominated Supreme Court declared most of these programs unconstitutional. These Court decisions angered President Roosevelt. He attempted to reform the judiciary. President Roosevelt's 1937 congressional proposal would have increased the president's power to appoint an additional judge to the federal judiciary, including to the Supreme Court, for every judge who had reached the age of seventy but declined to retire. This plan would have enabled Roosevelt to appoint an additional six justices to the Supreme Court.

Roosevelt's judiciary reform became known as "court packing." The press criticized it and compared the president to a dictator. Congress refused to increase the membership of the Supreme Court to fifteen members. Ironically, time would do what Roosevelt's "court packing" could not. By 1941, four Supreme Court justices had retired and two more had died. In total,

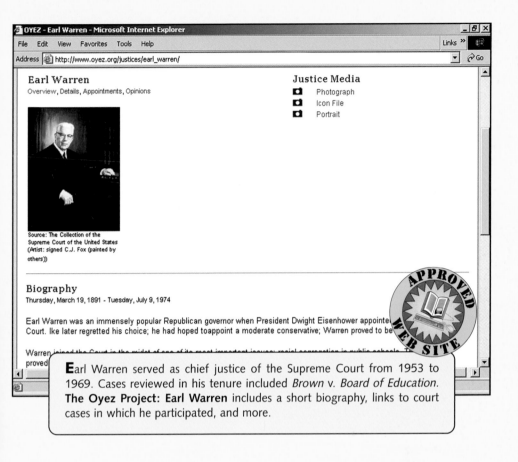

Earl Warren
Overview, Details, Appointments, Opinions

Justice Media
- Photograph
- Icon File
- Portrait

Source: The Collection of the
Supreme Court of the United States
(Artist: signed C.J. Fox (painted by others))

Biography
Thursday, March 19, 1891 - Tuesday, July 9, 1974

Earl Warren was an immensely popular Republican governor when President Dwight Eisenhower appointe
Court. Ike later regretted his choice; he had hoped to appoint a moderate conservative; Warren proved to be

Warren joined the Court in the midst of one of its most important issues: racial segregation in public schools. T
proved

Earl Warren served as chief justice of the Supreme Court from 1953 to 1969. Cases reviewed in his tenure included *Brown* v. *Board of Education*. **The Oyez Project: Earl Warren** includes a short biography, links to court cases in which he participated, and more.

seven of the nine justices on the Court were ultimately Roosevelt appointees.[6]

⚖ EARL WARREN AND CIVIL LIBERTIES

During the Warren period, the Court enlarged civil liberties and removed many of the constitutional restraints on the regulation of the economy. Civil liberties are constitutionally guaranteed rights of individuals. The major source of these liberties is the Bill of Rights. The Bill of Rights refers to the first ten amendments to the

Constitution. The Supreme Court gave the most support to civil liberties in the 1960s. The emphasis by the Court on civil liberties came because of changes in its membership. An important change in membership occurred when President Dwight Eisenhower appointed Earl Warren as the new Chief Justice in 1953. The Court's policies during this period are often identified with Warren, but justices Hugo Black, William Douglas, and William Brennan played roles of equal importance. Few periods in the history of the Supreme Court have been as active in making decisions affecting individual rights as that of the Warren Court. The Warren Court spanned from 1953 to 1969.

⚖ *Brown*

The most important decision of the Warren Court was *Brown* v. *Board of Education* in 1954. The Court declared segregation of schools that assigned students to school by race unconstitutional. The Court held that segregation of white and black students based on race denies black children the equal protection of the laws guaranteed by the Fourteenth Amendment. Thurgood Marshall, the lawyer who presented the *Brown* case to the Court, later became the first African-American Supreme Court justice. President Lyndon Johnson appointed Marshall to the Court

▲ *Thurgood Marshall was on the winning team of lawyers in the landmark case* Brown *vs.* Board of Education. *Years later, he became the first African-American justice on the Supreme Court.*

in 1957. Previously, Marshall served as solicitor general in the attorney general's office. The solicitor general is the attorney who represents or advises the federal government when it is involved in a lawsuit.

Marshall served twenty-three years on the Court. He was instrumental, along with the Court, in improving race relations in the twentieth century. Marshall also strongly supported equal protection under the law for women, children, prisoners, and the homeless. Marshall retired in 1991 at the age of eighty-two, and died a year later. Many legal scholars agree that Marshall had a career of remarkable accomplishment. Indeed, Marshall demonstrated, like many justices before him, that a single justice can have a large impact on the Court and country.

⚖ Rights of the Accused

During the 1960s, the Court also expanded the rights of criminal defendants. In the case of *Gideon* v. *Wainwright,* the Court required state governments to provide attorneys for those criminal defendants in serious criminal cases who cannot afford to hire their own. *Mapp* v. *Ohio* limited police search and seizure practices. *Miranda* v. *Arizona* establishes that accused individuals be given certain warnings before being questioned by police officers. The *Miranda* decision required

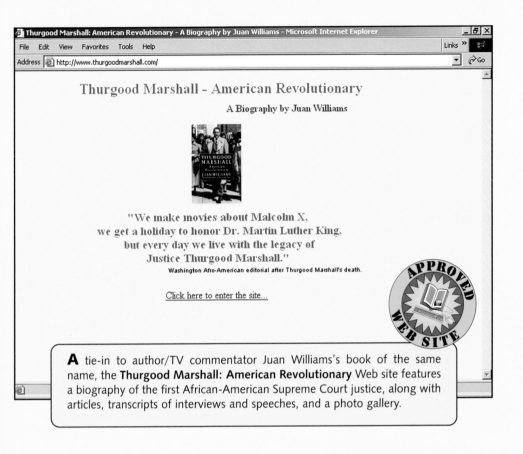

Thurgood Marshall: American Revolutionary - A Biography by Juan Williams - Microsoft Internet Explorer

File   Edit   View   Favorites   Tools   Help   Links »

Address 🔊 http://www.thurgoodmarshall.com/   ▼ ⌐ Go

Thurgood Marshall - American Revolutionary

A Biography by Juan Williams

"We make movies about Malcolm X,
we get a holiday to honor Dr. Martin Luther King,
but every day we live with the legacy of
Justice Thurgood Marshall."

Washington Afro-American editorial after Thurgood Marshall's death.

Click here to enter the site...

APPROVED WEB SITE

A tie-in to author/TV commentator Juan Williams's book of the same name, the **Thurgood Marshall: American Revolutionary** Web site features a biography of the first African-American Supreme Court justice, along with articles, transcripts of interviews and speeches, and a photo gallery.

that police inform suspects in custody of their right to remain silent and to an attorney. *Miranda* also requires police to advise suspects in custody that if they want to talk to police, what they say may later be used against them in court. In addition, the Court supported freedom of expression by expanding the First Amendment in the area of pornography and libel. So progressive was the Warren Court that conservatives posted billboards all over the United States urging Congress to "Impeach Earl Warren."

⚖ BURGER COURT

Chief Justice Earl Warren's retirement in 1969 gave President Richard Nixon the opportunity to choose Warren Burger as the new chief justice of Supreme Court. As Nixon hoped, the Burger Court turned out to be more conservative than the liberal Warren Court in some areas. In matters related to criminal justice, the Burger Court supported the constitutionality of the death penalty. With regard to civil liberties, the Court allowed local communities, not the federal government, to decide for themselves whether something was obscene. The Burger Court's most controversial decision was *Roe* v. *Wade*. The *Roe* v. *Wade* case held that women have a constitutional right to access an abortion during the first six months of pregnancy. This decision overturned some state abortion laws that had previously made it criminal to provide abortions.

With regard to civil rights issues, the Burger Court leaned toward being a liberal court. For example, the Court tended to approve affirmative action programs. Affirmative action states that employers, when hiring, in order to remedy past discrimination, should give preferential treatment to minority applicants. That is, if a minority applicant and white applicant were otherwise equal, the minority applicant would be hired. In *Bakke* v. *University of California at Davis,* the Court

Warren Burger served as chief justice of the Supreme Court during important cases such as *Roe* v. *Wade*, *Dole* v. *Bolton*, and the *University of California* v. *Bakke*. The **Warren E. Burger Online Exhibit** from the College of William and Mary provides more info about his life and career.

supported the use of affirmative action in order to remedy what seemed to be racial imbalances in education.

One of the most notable decisions of the Burger Court came in the case of *United States* v. *Nixon* in 1974. The Court was called on to decide whether President Nixon had to turn his White House tapes over to the courts. The tapes involved Nixon's phone conversations in the Oval Office of the White House. The special prosecutor in the Watergate scandal sought these tapes to determine Nixon's involvement in it. When Nixon refused, the special prosecutor asked the Court for help. The Court unanimously ordered Nixon to turn over the tapes. This Court decision hastened the president's resignation in August 1974.[7]

THE REHNQUIST COURT

President Nixon appointed William Rehnquist to the Supreme Court in 1971. President Ronald Reagan later promoted Rehnquist to chief justice of the Supreme Court in 1986. Rehnquist remained chief justice until he died in 2005. During his term, the Court was dominated by conservatives. One liberal member of the Court, Harry Blackmun, went on to declare that the Supreme Court was "moving to the right . . . where it wants to go, by hood or by crook."[8] Many of the Warren and Burger Court decisions in the areas of criminal procedure and civil liberties were scaled back.

The Rehnquist Court also revived the concept of state sovereignty. That is, prior to the Rehnquist Court, the states were left with limited rights to challenge federal power. However, the Rehnquist Court began to restore the view that states have the right to resist some forms of federal action. *United States* v. *Lopez* is an example of the revival of state sovereignty. When Congress passed a bill that forbade anyone from carrying a gun near a school, the Court held that carrying guns did not affect interstate commerce. The Court declared the law was unacceptable. In another Supreme Court case, *Alden* v. *Maine,* the Rehnquist Court held that the Brady gun control law could be used to require local law enforcement officers to do background checks on people trying to buy weapons.

In 1999, Rehnquist became the second chief justice (after Salmon P. Chase) to preside over a presidential impeachment trial. The chief justice presides over impeachment trials before the Senate.

▲ *In this image, Chief Justice Rehnquist takes his oath after being promoted from associate justice to chief justice by President Reagan.*

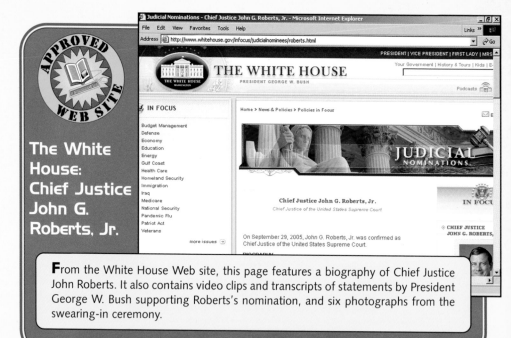

Judicial Nominations - Chief Justice John G. Roberts, Jr. - Microsoft Internet Explorer

File Edit View Favorites Tools Help

Links »

Address http://www.whitehouse.gov/infocus/judicialnominees/roberts.html

PRESIDENT | VICE PRESIDENT | FIRST LADY | MRS

THE WHITE HOUSE
PRESIDENT GEORGE W. BUSH

Your Government | History & Tours | Kids | E-

Podcasts

IN FOCUS

Budget Management
Defense
Economy
Education
Energy
Gulf Coast
Health Care
Homeland Security
Immigration
Iraq
Medicare
National Security
Pandemic Flu
Patriot Act
Veterans

more issues

Home > News & Policies > Policies in Focus

JUDICIAL
NOMINATIONS

Chief Justice John G. Roberts, Jr.
Chief Justice of the United States Supreme Court

IN FOCUS

CHIEF JUSTICE
JOHN G. ROBERTS,

On September 29, 2005, John G. Roberts, Jr. was confirmed as
Chief Justice of the United States Supreme Court.

The White House: Chief Justice John G. Roberts, Jr.

From the White House Web site, this page features a biography of Chief Justice John Roberts. It also contains video clips and transcripts of statements by President George W. Bush supporting Roberts's nomination, and six photographs from the swearing-in ceremony.

Access this Web site from http://www.myreportlinks.com

⚖ THE CURRENT COURT

John Roberts became the seventeenth chief justice when he took the oath of office on September 29, 2005. So far, Roberts has been a reliable conservative vote. Judicial scholars consider him a "cautious conservative." On January 17, 2006, the Roberts Court decided its first case. In *Gonzales* v. *Oregon,* the Court held that an Oregon state law permitting doctor-assisted suicide did not violate the Constitution. Chief Justice Roberts voted with the minority.[9]

IMPORTANT PEOPLE IN THE COURTS

4

There are several categories of individuals associated with the judiciary. They include past and present chief justices of the Supreme Court, associate justices of the Supreme Court, and the Supreme Court law clerks.

⚖ CHIEF JUSTICE

The chief justice of the Supreme Court is head of the judicial branch of the United States government. Since 1789, seventeen chief justices have been on the United States Supreme Court. Among the ranks are an ex-president, the United States chief prosecutor at Nuremberg Nazi War Crimes

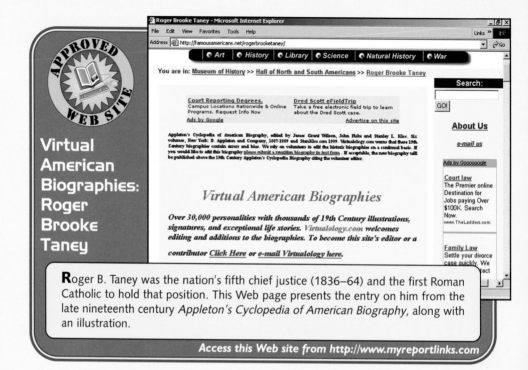

Virtual American Biographies: Roger Brooke Taney

Roger B. Taney was the nation's fifth chief justice (1836–64) and the first Roman Catholic to hold that position. This Web page presents the entry on him from the late nineteenth century *Appleton's Cyclopedia of American Biography*, along with an illustration.

Access this Web site from http://www.myreportlinks.com

Trial, and former governors from the states of New York and California. John G. Roberts is the seventeenth chief justice of the United States. Like other members of the judiciary, the president appoints chief justices and the Senate confirms them. Congress sets the salary of the chief justice. It was set at $212,100 a year as of 2007.[1]

⚖ DUTIES

The chief justice presides over impeachment trials of the president of the United States in the Senate. This is based on Article I, Section 3 of the Constitution. Two chief justices have had the opportunity to do so. Chief Justice Salmon

P. Chase presided over the impeachment trial of President Andrew Johnson in 1868. Andrew Johnson served as the president from 1865 to 1869. The Senate failed to convict Johnson by a single vote. In 1974, the House Judiciary Committee passed articles of impeachment against President Nixon. He resigned before the House of Representatives voted on those articles of impeachment. Chief Justice William Rehnquist presided over President Bill Clinton's impeachment trial in the Senate. Like Johnson, the Senate lacked the sufficient vote against President Clinton.[2]

▲ *This is a replica of the tickets handed out for admittance to President Andrew Johnson's impeachment trial.*

Another important duty of the chief justice is to administer the oath of office to the president of the United States. The oath is specified in Article II, Section 1 of the Constitution. The ailing Chief Justice William Rehnquist administered the oath to President George W. Bush on January 20, 2005. Rehnquist died in September of the same year.

⚖️ SENIORITY

The chief justice is considered the justice with the most authority. He is the senior member

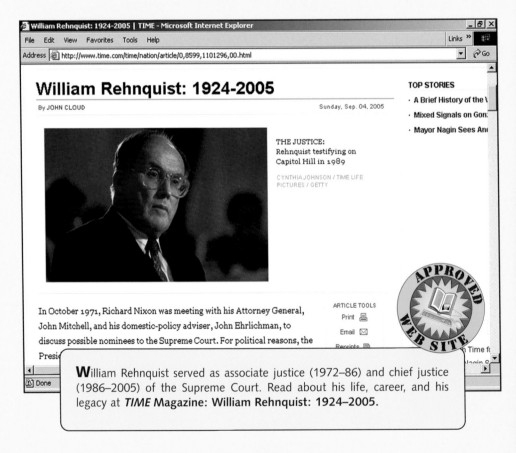

William Rehnquist served as associate justice (1972–86) and chief justice (1986–2005) of the Supreme Court. Read about his life, career, and his legacy at *TIME* Magazine: William Rehnquist: 1924–2005.

regardless of the number of years he has served as the chief justice. As the senior member of the Supreme Court, he leads the discussion when cases are discussed and heard. Seniority gives the chief justice great influence in framing the discussion. If he votes with the majority, the chief justice will decide which justice will write the opinion of the Court.

⚖ JOHN JAY

John Jay served as the first chief justice of the Supreme Court from 1789 to 1794. Before he was chief justice, Jay served as a delegate in the First and Second Continental Congresses. In 1780, he became United States ambassador to Spain. He was also a delegate to the Peace of Paris. The Peace of Paris officially ended the American Revolution in 1783. In addition, John Jay was one of the authors of the *Federalist Papers*. It consists of newspapers articles, which were written in support of the ratification of the United States Constitution in 1787. Jay's public career ended as the governor of New York from 1795 to 1801.

Besides establishing rules and procedures of the Supreme Court, the Jay Court reviewed several cases. In *Chisholm v. Georgia* (1793), the Court held it was constitutional for a private citizen in one state to sue another state in federal

▲ Chief Justice John Jay

John Jay Papers - Columbia University Libraries - Microsoft Internet Explorer

File   Edit   View   Favorites   Tools   Help   Links »

Address   http://www.columbia.edu/cu/lweb/digital/jay/

COLUMBIA UNIVERSITY LIBRARIES

The Papers of John Jay

The Papers of John Jay is an image database and indexing tool comprising some 13,000 documents (more than 30,000 page images) scanned chiefly from photocopies of original documents. Most of the source material was assembled by Columbia University's John Jay publication project staff during the 1960s and 1970s under the direction of the late Professor Richard B. Morris.
More about the project >>

Search

Background Material

+ Biographical Essay
+ Jay and the Constitution
+ Jay and New York
+ The Jay Treaty
+ Jay and France
+ Jay and Slavery
+ Jay Print Project
+ Legacy Conference

About the Project

+ History & Description
+ Source Collections
+ Bibliography
+ Rights a
+ Parti
+ Ne

APPROVED WEB SITE

John Jay was the first Supreme Court chief justice, serving from 1789 to 1794. He was also one of the authors of the *Federalist Papers*. **The Papers of John Jay** Web site features a large collection of scans of his writings (with introductions), plus background essays and a bibliography.

court. This decision of the Court made many Anti-Federalists mad. The decision was overturned through the adoption of the Eleventh Amendment in 1795. It states that a citizen of another state, without the state's permission, cannot sue the state in federal court.

As John Jay prepared for retirement, President John Adams asked him if he would be interested in returning to the Court. Jay refused the offer. John Adams appointed John Marshall to fill the vacancy. Marshall replaced Chief Justice Oliver Ellsworth who had retired in 1800.[3]

⚖ JOHN MARSHALL

John Marshall served as the secretary of state in President John Adams's Cabinet prior to becoming the fourth chief justice of the Supreme Court in 1801. He served a record thirty-four years and through the administration of six presidents. John Marshall participated in more than one thousand decisions and wrote over five hundred opinions of the Court. During his term, the Court began issuing single majority opinions, instead of multiple ones. This new procedure enabled the Court to speak with a unified voice. The Court's most significant rulings supported the dominance of federal power over the states. Justice Marshall helped establish the Supreme Court as the final authority on the meaning of the Constitution.

Marshall's decisions continue to guide the Supreme Court and the United States government today. The Marshall Court established the principle of judicial review in the 1803 case of *Marbury v. Madison*. Based on this principle, the Supreme Court can declare invalid any act of federal or state government that is in conflict with the United States Constitution.[4]

▲ Chief Justice John Marshall

⚖ ROGER BROOKE TANEY

President Andrew Jackson appointed Roger Taney in 1836. He was the fifth chief justice of the Supreme Court. He presided over the Court for twenty-eight years until his death in 1864. *Dred Scott* v. *Sandford* is the case most closely associated with Taney's Court. Dred Scott held that slaves were not citizens. In addition, slaves could not sue in the courts. Moreover, the Court ruled that Congress could not forbid slavery in the territories of the United States. This decision inflicted enormous injury to the Court as an institution. The decision made the Civil War inevitable. It took the Court at least a generation to recover.[5]

⚖ WILLIAM HOWARD TAFT

William Howard Taft is the only president who also served as chief justice. Taft became the twenty-seventh president in 1908. The Republican Party renominated him, but he lost the election to Woodrow Wilson in 1912. President Warren G. Harding selected Taft to replace Chief Justice Edward White in 1921. Taft served as chief justice until 1930.

Taft's major achievement on the Court has to do with his administrative ability. He was able to reduce the Court's crowded schedule. He did it by securing the passage of the Judiciary Act of 1925. This act allows the Supreme Court to determine

▲ Chief Justice William Howard Taft (left) administered the oath of office to President Herbert Hoover on March 4, 1929. Taft himself, had served as the twenty-seventh president of the United States.

its own appellate jurisdiction. Taft also convinced Congress that the Court should have its own building. However, Taft did not live to see the building's completion. He died several months after he retired from the Court in 1930.[6]

Current Members
of the Supreme Court

⚖ CHIEF JUSTICE JOHN G. ROBERTS, JR.

John Roberts was born in New York on January 27, 1955. As of 2007, Roberts was the youngest member of the Supreme Court. He received his law degree from Harvard Law School in 1979. He served as a law clerk for Henry J. Friendly of the United States Court of Appeals for the Second Circuit from 1979 to 1980. He also served as a law clerk for then Associate Justice William H. Rehnquist of the Supreme Court of the United States in 1980. President George W. Bush appointed Roberts to the United States Court of Appeals for the District of Columbia in 2003. President Bush later nominated him as chief justice of the United States. Roberts took his seat as the seventeenth chief justice on September 29, 2005. He sides with conservative issues.

⚖ JOHN PAUL STEVENS

In 2007, John Paul Stevens was the most experienced member of the Supreme Court in both service and age. He was born in Chicago, Illinois, on April 20, 1920. He received his undergraduate degree from the University of Chicago, and his law degree from Northwestern University. Stevens was a law clerk to Supreme Court Justice Wiley Rutledge in 1947. From 1970–75, Stevens served as a judge of the United States Court of Appeals for

▲ The Supreme Court as it appeared in 2007. Standing left to right are Stephen G. Breyer, Clarence Thomas, Ruth Bader Ginsburg, and Samuel Alito, Jr. Seated left to right are Anthony M. Kennedy, John Paul Stevens, Chief Justice John G. Roberts, Jr., Antonin Scalia, and David H. Souter.

the Seventh Circuit. President Gerald R. Ford nominated Stevens as an associate justice of the Supreme Court, and he took his seat December 19, 1975. He has been a consistent liberal.

⚖ ANTONIN SCALIA

Antonin Scalia was born in Trenton, New Jersey, on March 11, 1936. He received his undergraduate degree from Georgetown University and the University of Freiberg in Switzerland, and his law degree from Harvard Law School. Scalia taught

▲ President Ronald Reagan speaks with Supreme Court justice Antonin Scalia. Reagan nominated Scalia to the Court.

law at the University of Virginia and the University of Chicago from 1967 to 1982. He was appointed federal judge of the United States Court of Appeals for the District of Columbia Circuit in 1982. President Reagan nominated Scalia as an associate justice of the Supreme Court, and he took his seat on September 26, 1986. He is considered a consistent conservative.

⚖ ANTHONY M. KENNEDY

Anthony M. Kennedy was born in Sacramento, California, on July 23, 1936. He received his undergraduate degree from Stanford University and the London School of Economics, and his law degree from Harvard Law School. From 1965 to 1988, Kennedy was a professor of constitutional law at the McGeorge School of Law at the University of the Pacific. He was appointed to the United States Court of Appeals for the Ninth Circuit in 1975. President Ronald Reagan nominated Kennedy as an associate justice of the Supreme Court, and he joined the Court on February 18, 1988. Kennedy was President Reagan's third nominee to fill this particular seat. The Senate did not confirm Reagan's first nominee, Robert Bork. Douglas Ginsburg was Reagan's second appointee, but he withdrew his name. Anthony Kennedy is considered a moderate member of the Court.

Associate Justice David Souter took his seat on the Supreme Court on October 9, 1990.

⚖ DAVID HACKETT SOUTER

David Souter was born in Melrose, Massachusetts, on September 17, 1939. He became a Rhodes Scholar at Oxford University in Great Britain. Souter received his law degree from Harvard Law School. He became the attorney general of New Hampshire in 1976. He was a judge on the United States Court of Appeals for the First Circuit in 1990. President George H. W. Bush nominated him as an associate justice of the Supreme Court in 1990. Although appointed by a conservative president, Souter remains a consistent liberal on the Court.

⚖ CLARENCE THOMAS

Clarence Thomas was born in the Pin Point community of Georgia on June 23, 1948. He attended Conception Seminary and received his undergraduate degree from the College of the Holy

Cross. Thomas received his law degree from Yale Law School in 1974. He served as legislative assistant to Senator John Danforth of Missouri from 1979 until 1981. From 1981 to 1982, Thomas served as assistant secretary for civil rights in the United States Department of Education. He became the chairman of the U.S. Equal Employment Opportunity Commission in 1982. He became a judge of the United States Court of Appeals for the District of Columbia Circuit in 1990. President George H. W. Bush nominated him as an associate justice of the Supreme Court in 1991. Clarence Thomas is the second African-American justice to sit on the Supreme Court. The first African-American justice appointed to the Court was Thurgood Marshall. Thomas remains a consistent conservative member of the Court.

President George H. W. Bush ▶ nominated Clarence Thomas to the Supreme Court in 1991. He is just the second African American to have served on the Court.

⚖ RUTH BADER GINSBURG

Ruth Bader Ginsburg was born in Brooklyn, New York, on March 15, 1933. She received her under-graduate degree from Cornell University. She obtained her law degree from Columbia Law School. Ginsburg was a professor of law at Rut-gers University School of Law from 1963–72, and Columbia Law School from 1972 until 1980. In 1971, she was instrumental in launching the Women's Rights Project of the American Civil Liberties Union (ACLU). She served as the ACLU's General Counsel from 1973 to 1980. Ginsburg also served on the ACLU's National Board of Directors from 1974 until 1980. She was appointed a judge on the United States Court of Appeals for the District of Columbia Circuit in 1980. President Bill Clinton nominated her as an associate justice of the Supreme Court in 1993. She is the second woman to serve on the Supreme Court. Sandra Day O'Connor was the first female member of the Court. Ruth Bader Ginsburg has consistently supported liberal issues and causes on the Court.

⚖ STEPHEN G. BREYER

Stephen Breyer was born in San Francisco, California, on August 15, 1938. He received his undergraduate degree from Stanford University and his law degree from Harvard Law School. He

▲ *President Clinton looks on as Chief Justice Rehnquist swears in Ruth Bader Ginsburg.*

served as a law clerk to Justice Arthur Goldberg of the Supreme Court of the United States in 1964. Breyer was the chief counsel of the Senate Judiciary Committee from 1979 to 1980. He was also an assistant professor at Harvard Law School from 1967 to 1994 and a professor at the Harvard University Kennedy School of Government from 1977 to 1980. From 1980 to 1990, he served as a judge of the United States Court of Appeals for the First Circuit. President Clinton nominated Breyer as an

▲ Samuel A. Alito joined the Supreme Court in January 2006. In this photo, Alito is clutching the Carol Los Mansmann Award for Distinguished Public Service after receiving the honor on April 4, 2007.

associate justice of the Supreme Court in 1994. Stephen Breyer is a liberal-leaning member on the Court.

⚖ SAMUEL ANTHONY ALITO, JR.

Samuel Alito is the newest member of the Supreme Court. He was born in Trenton, New Jersey, on April 1, 1950. He received his under-graduate degree from Princeton University in 1972 and his law degree from Yale Law School in 1975. He was appointed to the United States Court of Appeals for the Third Circuit in 1990. President George W. Bush nominated him as an associate justice of the Supreme Court, and Alito took his seat on January 31, 2006. He is consid-ered a conservative.

⚖ SANDRA DAY O'CONNOR (RECENTLY RETIRED)

Sandra Day O'Connor was born in El Paso, Texas, on March 26, 1930. She received both her under-graduate and law degree from Stanford University. She was appointed to the Arizona State Senate in 1969 and was subsequently reelected to two two-year terms. In 1975, O'Connor was elected judge of the Maricopa County Superior Court and served until 1979, when she was appointed to the Arizona Court of Appeals. President Reagan nominated her as an associate justice of the

Now retired, Sandra Day O'Connor served on the Supreme Court from 1981 to 2006. She was the first woman to serve on the Court.

Supreme Court, and she took her seat on September 25, 1981. O'Connor was the first woman to serve on the Supreme Court. Justice O'Connor retired from the Supreme Court on January 31, 2006, but remains active in government service.[7]

⚖ LAW CLERKS

Law clerks are recent graduates of mainly well-known and prestigious law schools. The clerkship gives recent graduates of law schools hands-on experience in the judicial process. Clerkship positions are very competitive. They are traditionally awarded to law students who were very successful during college and law school. There are over two thousand law clerks working for federal judges.[8] Each member of the Supreme Court has between two and four law clerks. Law clerks perform a wide range of tasks. They help justices decide which cases should be heard by the Supreme

From the newest law clerk to the most experienced Supreme Court justice, each member of the federal judicial system works to ensure that America's laws are both fair and constitutional. That way, the "scales of justice" are balanced for all United States citizens.

Court. Specifically, law clerks draft memorandums. A typical memo summarizes the facts of the case, the questions of the law presented, and the recommended course of action. That is, they write up a recommendation on whether the case should be granted a full hearing or dismissed. Finally, once the Supreme Court hears a case, law clerks help to draft and court opinions.[9]

WHAT DOES THE JUDICIARY DO TODAY?

5

An important function of the judiciary is to interpret and apply the law. However, judges may influence policy when they perform this function. Members of Congress try to only make laws that they believe the Supreme Court will find constitutional. The courts' decisions affect a large part of our society. When the Supreme Court ruled in *Engel* v. *Vitale* (1962) that prayer in public school violated the Constitution, the Court influenced laws in some states. There are several ways the courts influences policy makers: through interpreting the Constitution, interpreting laws, overruling its past decisions, and imposing remedies.

However, the power of the courts to make policy presents difficulties for democracy. In a democracy, the power to make policies belongs to elected representatives. Yet court decisions affect policy far beyond the interests of those who are directly involved.

⚖ CONSTITUTIONAL INTERPRETATION

Former Supreme Court Justice Felix Frankfurter offers the following reasoning:

> The meaning of *due process* and the content of the terms like *liberty* are not revealed by the

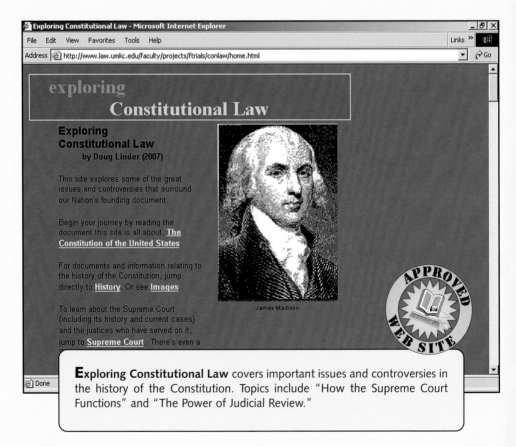

Exploring Constitutional Law covers important issues and controversies in the history of the Constitution. Topics include "How the Supreme Court Functions" and "The Power of Judicial Review."

Constitution. The justices make the meaning. They read into the neutral language of the Constitution their own economic and social views. . . . Let us face the fact that five Justices of the Supreme Court are the molders of policy rather than the impersonal vehicles of revealed truth."[1]

Thus, the vagueness of the Constitution means that it cannot be applied automatically. Different provisions must be interpreted. Constitutional interpretation is the specific way the judges understand the phrasing of the Constitution.

For more than two centuries, judges and scholars have debated the proper method of interpreting the Constitution. Interpreting the Constitution depends on a judge's philosophy of constitutional interpretation. There are two broad philosophies, an enduring document and a living document.[2]

⚖ ORIGINAL INTENT

The supporters of this philosophy interpret the Constitution to mean what the Founders intended it to mean. They often return to the *Federalist Papers* and other writings of the Founders to understand their intended meaning of the Constitution. *The Federalist Papers* consists of eighty-five different newspaper articles written by three Founders: Alexander Hamilton, James Madison, and John Jay. *The Federalist Papers*

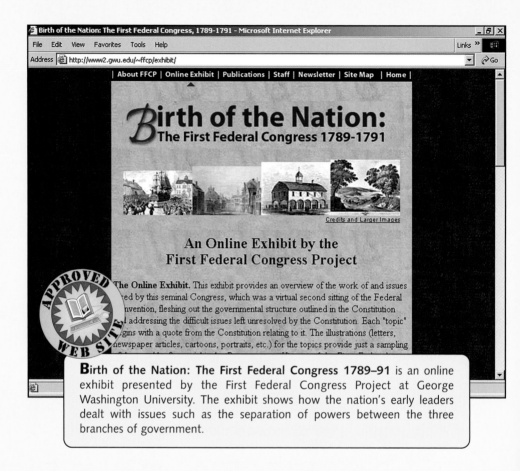

Birth of the Nation: The First Federal Congress 1789-1791 - Microsoft Internet Explorer

File   Edit   View   Favorites   Tools   Help   Links »

Address http://www2.gwu.edu/~ffcp/exhibit/   Go

| About FFCP | Online Exhibit | Publications | Staff | Newsletter | Site Map | Home |

Birth of the Nation:
The First Federal Congress 1789-1791

Credits and Larger Images

An Online Exhibit by the
First Federal Congress Project

The Online Exhibit. This exhibit provides an overview of the work of and issues ...ed by this seminal Congress, which was a virtual second sitting of the Federal ...nvention, fleshing out the governmental structure outlined in the Constitution ...l addressing the difficult issues left unresolved by the Constitution. Each "topic" ...gins with a quote from the Constitution relating to it. The illustrations (letters, ...ewspaper articles, cartoons, portraits, etc.) for the topics provide just a sampling

Birth of the Nation: The First Federal Congress 1789–91 is an online exhibit presented by the First Federal Congress Project at George Washington University. The exhibit shows how the nation's early leaders dealt with issues such as the separation of powers between the three branches of government.

elaborates on different parts of the Constitution. The supporters of this philosophy also stick to the meanings of the actual words used in the Constitution and the amendments. They do not try to interfere with the Founders' intent behind the words.

⚖A LIVING DOCUMENT

The supporters of this philosophy look at the Constitution as a "living" document. They argue that the founding fathers wrote the Constitution to be applied to all ages and all times. They believe that the document should be broadly interpreted in order to ensure its relevance to contemporary society.

The above two different philosophies of interpreting the Constitution can lead to different outcomes. The abortion decision in *Roe* v. *Wade* by the Supreme Court is an example of a "living document" reading. "Enduring document" supporters find no right to abortion. On the other hand, the decision of the Supreme Court upholding the death penalty exemplifies the "enduring document" philosophy. Only a broad reading of the Constitution would make capital punishment unconstitutional.

⚖ JUDICIAL REVIEW

Judicial review permits judges to invalidate laws enacted by legislatures, by declaring that these actions violated the Constitution. Both federal and state courts can exercise this power, but all lower court decisions involving federal law are subject to review by the Supreme Court. In reality, judicial review gives judges the power to reject laws passed by the representatives of people in Congress. This caused one senator, George W. Norris, to complain, "The people can change Congress but only God can change the Supreme Court."[3]

George W. Norris served as a Nebraska congressman and senator for over forty years. He had some insightful comments about the powers of the Supreme Court.

The Supreme Court first asserted its power of judicial review in the case of *Marbury* v. *Madison* in 1803. In a unanimous decision written by Chief Justice John Marshall, the Court declared Section 13 of the Judiciary Act of 1789 in violation of Article III of the United States Constitution. Federal courts have frequently used this in the twentieth century to strike down hundreds of state laws and more than one hundred acts of Congress.

For instance, in *Buckley* v. *Valeo* (1976), the Court struck down provisions of the Federal Campaign Act of 1974, deciding that the act was in violation of the First Amendment freedom of speech. Parts of the act had limited the amount individual candidates could spend to finance their own campaigns.[4]

⚖ OVERRULING ITSELF

The Supreme Court also affects policy by overruling itself. Although the court generally sticks to its past decisions, it has sometimes overruled its past decisions. The court has overruled itself in more than 140 cases since 1810. *Brown* v. *Board of Education* (1954), for example, overruled *Plessy* v. *Ferguson* (1896). The Court changed its position on racial segregation that it endorsed in *Plessy* v. *Ferguson* by declaring the decision to be in violation of the Constitution.

⚖ IMPOSING REMEDIES

Finally, judges also influence policymakers by the kinds of remedies they impose. A remedy is a judicial order that states what must be done to correct a situation. Today, the remedies imposed by the judges often apply to large groups. An example is *Ruiz* v. *Estelle* (1980). William Wayne Justice, a federal district court judge in Tyler, Texas, heard the case. Inmate David Ruiz sued the director of the Texas Department of Correction, William Estelle, in 1972. The charges included prison overcrowding and inadequate security and health care. The judge in this case issued an order not only to improve the lot of Ruiz, but also to

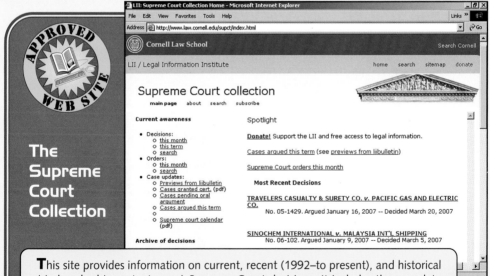

This site provides information on current, recent (1992–to present), and historical (six hundred important cases) Supreme Court decisions. It includes the complete text of recent decisions, plus summaries of recent court orders.

Access this Web site from http://www.myreportlinks.com

Supreme Court of the United States

No. 1 ———— , *October Term, 19* 54

Oliver Brown, Mrs. Richard Lawton, Mrs. Sadie Emmanuel et al.,

Appellants,

vs.

Board of Education of Topeka, Shawnee County, Kansas, et al.

Appeal from *the United States District Court for the* ————————————— *District of* Kansas.

This cause *came on to be heard on the transcript of the record from the United States District Court for the* ——————— *District of* Kansas, ——————— *and was argued by counsel.*

On consideration whereof, *It is ordered and adjudged by this Court that the judgment of the said* District ——————————— *Court in this cause be, and the same is hereby,* reversed with costs; and that this cause be, and the same is hereby, remanded to the said District Court to take such proceedings and enter such orders and decrees consistent with the opinions of this Court as are necessary and proper to admit to public schools on a racially nondiscriminatory basis with all deliberate speed the parties to this case.

Per Mr. Chief Justice Warren,

May 31, 1955.

E.W.

improve the entire prison system. The judge's decision was based on his interpretation of the Eighth Amendment, which prohibits cruel and unusual punishment. The result was an improvement in the living conditions of many prisoners in Texas. This improvement cost the state of Texas over $2 billion.

⚖ RESOLVING DISPUTES

The majority of the cases heard in the federal courts have little to do with the courts' policymaking. In most cases, the courts simply apply a settled body of laws to specific cases to resolve specific controversies. Courts try people accused of bankruptcy, resolve disputes over contracts, hear personal injury cases, and apply the patent law.

⚖ PARTIES IN DISPUTES

In most lawsuits, the parties are the plaintiff and the defendant. The plaintiff is the person or organization that starts the lawsuit. The defendant is the person or organization that is being sued. There may be more than one person or organization in a single lawsuit. Interest groups are examples of organizations. Interest groups are like-minded individuals who organize to affect government decisions. Interest groups either sue or assist in suing cases. Interest groups sue in

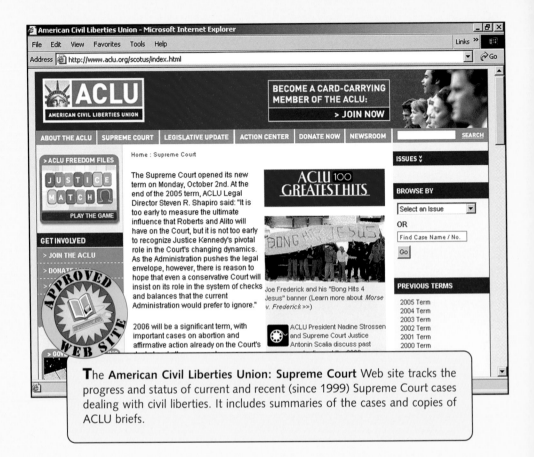

American Civil Liberties Union - Microsoft Internet Explorer

File   Edit   View   Favorites   Tools   Help   Links »

Address http://www.aclu.org/scotus/index.html   Go

BECOME A CARD-CARRYING
MEMBER OF THE ACLU:
> JOIN NOW

ABOUT THE ACLU   SUPREME COURT   LEGISLATIVE UPDATE   ACTION CENTER   DONATE NOW   NEWSROOM   SEARCH

> ACLU FREEDOM FILES   Home : Supreme Court

JUSTICE
MATCH   The Supreme Court opened its new
PLAY THE GAME   term on Monday, October 2nd. At the
                         end of the 2005 term, ACLU Legal
GET INVOLVED   Director Steven R. Shapiro said: "It is
                         too early to measure the ultimate
> JOIN THE ACLU   influence that Roberts and Alito will
                         have on the Court, but it is not too early
> DONATE   to recognize Justice Kennedy's pivotal
                         role in the Court's changing dynamics.
                         As the Administration pushes the legal
                         envelope, however, there is reason to
                         hope that even a conservative Court will
                         insist on its role in the system of checks
                         and balances that the current
                         Administration would prefer to ignore."

                         2006 will be a significant term, with
                         important cases on abortion and
                         affirmative action already on the Court's

ACLU 100
GREATEST HITS

Joe Frederick and his "Bong Hits 4
Jesus" banner (Learn more about *Morse
v. Frederick* >>)

ACLU President Nadine Strossen
and Supreme Court Justice
Antonin Scalia discuss past

ISSUES

BROWSE BY

Select an Issue

OR

Find Case Name / No.

Go

PREVIOUS TERMS

2005 Term
2004 Term
2003 Term
2002 Term
2001 Term
2000 Term

The **American Civil Liberties Union: Supreme Court** Web site tracks the
progress and status of current and recent (since 1999) Supreme Court cases
dealing with civil liberties. It includes summaries of the cases and copies of
ACLU briefs.

almost all civil liberties cases. For example, in
ACLU v. *NSA* (2006), the American Civil Liberties
Union filed a lawsuit against the National Security Agency (NSA). It was an attempt to end the
Bush administration's illegal spying on Americans. The NSA is a secretive government agency
which attempts to monitor information that could
help defend against an attack on the United
States. The lawsuit was filed on behalf of a group
of journalists, scholars, attorneys, and nonprofit

groups. They frequently communicate by phone and e-mail abroad.

Interest groups also file *amicus curiae* briefs, or "friend of the court" briefs. In the case of *Harris* v. *Forklift Systems* (1993), over thirty different interest groups filed amicus briefs. In the above, the Supreme Court unanimously ruled that Title VII of the Civil Rights Act was violated when Teresa Harris's supervisor subjected her to sexual harassment.

CLASS-ACTION SUITS

Sometimes, individuals and groups will bring a class-action suit. The suit is brought on behalf of a large group of people who have a common in-terest. *Dukes* v. *Wal-Mart Stores, Inc.* (2004), is the largest class-action suit in United States history. It charges Wal-Mart, the nation's largest retail chain, with discrimination against female employees. Title VII of the 1964 Civil Rights Act protects workers against discrimination based on sex, race, religion, or national origin. The case represented approximately 1.6 million women employees of Wal-Mart nationwide. In June 2004, the federal district court certified the case. When a court "certifies" a class action, it allows the case to proceed. Wal-Mart appealed the decision to the Ninth Circuit Court of Appeals.

⚖ RULES OF PROCEDURES

The courts use specialized rules in going about their work. Judges do not investigate cases, question witnesses, or develop arguments themselves. The two parties in a dispute present arguments on each side. This is called an adversarial system. It is a method of judicial decision making in which the impartial judge hears the arguments and reviews evidence presented in a court by each side.

In addition to bringing a case to court, individuals or groups must have standing. "Standing" means that a law or action must directly harm them. To sue, plaintiffs must show

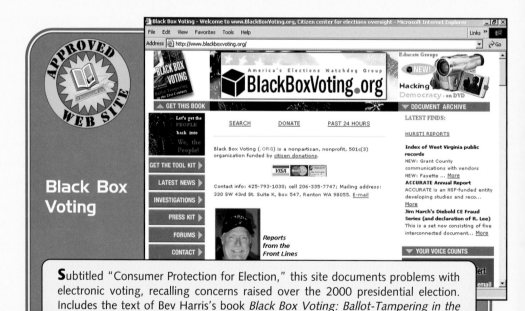

Black Box Voting

Subtitled "Consumer Protection for Election," this site documents problems with electronic voting, recalling concerns raised over the 2000 presidential election. Includes the text of Bev Harris's book *Black Box Voting: Ballot-Tampering in the 21st Century.*

Access this Web site from http://www.myreportlinks.com

they have suffered financial damages, loss of property, or physical or emotional harm because of an individual or group's action.

Going to court requires money. Criminal defendants are guaranteed an attorney, without charge if they are poor or if they are unable to provide one. In civil suits, the most common arrangement is the contingency fee. Here a plaintiff agrees to pay all expenses. If the plaintiff wins, he or she shares one third or more of the money damages with the lawyer. Lawyers do not participate in such arrangements unless they are certain that they will win.

⚖ AMERICA AND THE COURTS

America is a litigious society. There are more than 10 million civil disputes in the nation's courts each year. There are more than 800,000 lawyers compared to 650,000 physicians in the United States. These lawyers search for new legal principles on which to bring lawsuits. They expand the definition of civil wrongdoing in order to increase the threat of lawsuits.[5]

It is true that the threat of lawsuits protects us because the victims require compensation for actual damage. However, there are many frivolous lawsuits in America. Some lawsuits are brought without any basis. These lawsuits are initiated because individuals or groups will offer

These statues sit above the motto "Equal Justice Under Law" which is engraved above the main entrance of the Supreme Court building. The statue in the center is called Liberty Enthroned.

Independent Judiciary - Microsoft Internet Explorer

File   Edit   View   Favorites   Tools   Help   Links »

Address http://www.independentjudiciary.org/   Go

INDEPENDENT JUDICIARY

A PROJECT OF THE ALLIANCE FOR JUSTICE

EARTH IS OUR FUTURE

INDEPENDENT COURTS FOR ALL AMERICANS

☆ ABOUT US   ☆ ACTION CENTER   ☆ CONTRIBUTE   ☆ ISSUES   ☆ NEWS & EVENTS

THE NOMINATION PROCESS: ★ THE COURTS   ★ THE NOMINEES   ★ THE SENATE

Securing Access to Justice

WELCOME TO THE **ALLIANCE FOR JUSTICE**'s website, **IndependentJudiciary**, which provides current information and the latest news on nominations to the federal bench. The Alliance for Justice's Judicial Selection Project examines judicial nominations and encourages public participation in the confirmation process. Since 1985, Alliance for Justice has led the fight for a fair and independent judiciary. For more information about Alliance for Justice, visit **www.allianceforjustice.org**.

ALLIA

Sea
Selectio

Curre

The **Independent Judiciary** site is run by Alliance for Progress, which seeks to increase public participation in judicial selection. It contains biographies and career summaries of current federal nominees, a map of the circuits, and links to "Full Court Press" (covering court decisions) and "Justice Digest" (covering nominations).

a settlement to avoid the expenses of defending themselves.

Social costs of these frivolous suits are tremendous. For example, physicians order expensive tests and procedures to protect themselves from lawsuits. Insurance premiums have gone up not only for physicians, but also for recreational facilities, day-care centers, motels, and restaurants for similar reasons. For example, a woman who spilled hot coffee sued a fast-food restaurant for making the coffee too hot. In addition, the threat of lawsuits discourages companies from releasing new products into the marketplace.

Reforming our liability laws presents a major challenge to government. Some groups, like physicians, manufacturers, insurance companies, and hospitals, support and welcome reform. On the other hand, legal professionals, like the American Association for Justice, may resist any reform.

Report Links

The Internet sites described below can be accessed at
http://www.myreportlinks.com

▶**Supreme Court of the United States**
Editor's Choice Meet the justices of the Supreme Court, and learn more about its operations.

▶**Federal Judicial Center: History of the Federal Judiciary**
Editor's Choice Learn about the history of the federal judiciary system.

▶**Understanding the Federal Courts**
Editor's Choice More about the federal court system in the United States.

▶**PBS: The Supreme Court**
Editor's Choice Explore the history of the Supreme Court by selecting interactive timelines.

▶**The Supreme Court Historical Society**
Editor's Choice Find out about the history of the Supreme Court and its current operations.

▶**Ben's Guide to U.S. Government for Kids**
Editor's Choice Here's a way to understand how the Supreme Court works.

▶**American Civil Liberties Union: Supreme Court**
Read about the ACLU's involvement in Supreme Court cases affecting civil liberties.

▶**Birth of the Nation: The First Federal Congress 1789–91**
Learn how the framers of the Constitution dealt with issues such as the balance of powers.

▶**Black Box Voting**
See about the controversy over electronic voting machines and their potential flaws.

▶**C-SPAN.org: America and the Courts**
Browse the history of the court system on this Web site.

▶**Documents Related to the 2000 Election Dispute**
Learn all about the controversy surrounding the 2000 presidential election.

▶**Exploring Constitutional Law**
Explore issues and controversies in constitutional law.

▶**FindLaw: U.S. District Courts**
Quickly find information on District Courts in any portion of the United States.

▶**Independent Judiciary**
Read about efforts to increase public participation in the selection of federal judges.

▶**John Marshall House**
Learn about the history and career of Supreme Court Chief Justice John Marshall.

The Internet sites described below can be accessed at
http://www.myreportlinks.com

▶**National Center for State Courts**
Learn all about the state courts through this Web site, which seeks to help them operate.

▶**The Oyez Project: Earl Warren**
Read about Chief Justice Earl Warren and his involvement in *Brown* v. *Board of Education*.

▶**The Papers of John Jay**
Read the writings of the first Supreme Court chief justice.

▶**The Supreme Court Collection**
The Supreme Court through current, recent, and historical cases.

▶**Thurgood Marshall: American Revolutionary**
Learn about the life of Supreme Court Justice Thurgood Marshall.

▶*TIME* **Magazine: William Rehnquist: 1924–2005**
Learn about the life of Supreme Court Chief Justice William Rehnquist.

▶**United States Court of Appeals for the Federal Circuit**
Learn about the activities and decisions of the Federal Circuit Appeals Court.

▶**United States Court of Federal Claims**
Read about the operations of "The People's Court."

▶**United States Court of International Trade**
Read about the history and practices of the U.S. court devoted to international trade.

▶**United States Tax Court**
Find out what goes on in federal tax court.

▶**U.S. Court of Appeals for the Armed Forces**
Learn all about the history and operations of the U.S. Court of Appeals for the Armed Forces.

▶**U.S. Court of Appeals for Veterans Claims**
Learn about the operations of the federal court that deals with veterans' claims.

▶**Virtual American Biographies: Roger Brooke Taney**
A biography of Supreme Court Chief Justice Robert B. Taney.

▶**Warren E. Burger Online Exhibit**
Find out about the life of Supreme Court Chief Justice Warren Burger.

▶**The White House: Chief Justice John G. Roberts, Jr.**
Read about the life of Supreme Court Chief Justice John Roberts.

adversarial system—Method of judicial decision making in which the impartial judge/jury hears arguments and reviews evidence presented in a court by each side.

amicus curiae—A type of brief filed to the Supreme Court by an individual or organization who is not directly involved in a case.

appellate jurisdiction—The power of a court to review a case to determine whether a trial court correctly applied the law and followed established legal procedures.

chief justice—The presiding judge of the Supreme Court.

class action suit—A lawsuit brought on behalf of a large group of people who have common interest.

Court—When capitalized, the word "court" refers specifically to the Supreme Court of the United States.

court packing—President Franklin D. Roosevelt's unsuccessful attempt to increase the membership of the Supreme Court from 9 to 15.

defendant—An individual or organization who is being sued or charged with a crime.

en banc—A Latin phrase meaning with the full authority of the court.

judicial review—The power of a court, ultimately the Supreme Court, to determine whether a federal law is constitutional.

judiciary—One of the three branches of government that interprets and applies laws to cases to resolve disputes between individuals or groups.

jurisdiction—The power of a court to hear and decide a case.

law clerks—Recent graduates of law schools who help judges with their duties.

Memorandum—In law, a legal memo usually written by a law clerk regarding the specifics of a current or upcoming case.

original jurisdiction—The power of a court to hear and decide a case for the first time.

plaintiff—An individual or organization that begins a lawsuit.

Rule of Four—Four of the nine members of the Supreme Court must vote to accept a case to be reviewed.

writ of certiorari—A document filed by a party with the Supreme Court asking the Court to review the decision of a lower court.

written briefs—Detailed arguments of a case submitted to the Supreme Court by parties involved in a dispute.

Chapter 1. The United States Supreme Court and the Election of 2000

1. *"George W. Bush, et al., Petitioners* v. *Albert Gore, Jr., et al.,* On Writ of Certiorari to the Florida Supreme Court," FindLaw for Legal Professionals, December 12, 2000, <http://caselaw.lp.findlaw.com/scripts/getcase.pl?court=US&vol=000&invol=00-949> (May 15, 2006).

2. Alexis de Tocqueville, *Democracy in America* (New York: Mentor Books, 1956), p. 75.

Chapter 2. Organization and Responsibilities

1. "Supreme Court of United States," *supremecourtus.gov,* n.d., <http://www.supremecourtus.gov> (May 23, 2006).

2. Ibid.

3. "The Supreme Court of the United States," *Encyclopedia Britannica,* 2006, <http://www.britannica.com/eb/article-233789> (June 26, 2006).

4. Saul Brenner, "Granting Certiorari by the United States Supreme Court: An Overview of the Social Science Studies," *Law Library Journal,* 2000, <http://www.aallnet.org/products/2000-17pdf> (June 13, 2006).

5. *U.S. Court of Appeals for Federal Circuit,* May 24, 2006, <http://www.fedcir.gov> (June 15, 2006).

6. Robert A. Carp and Ronald Stidham, *The Federal Courts* (Washington, D.C.: Congressional Quarterly Press, 1998), pp. 28–30.

Chapter 3. History of the Judiciary

1. "History of the Federal Judiciary," *Federal Judiciary Center,* n.d., <http://www.fjc.gov/history/home.nsf> (June 11, 2006).

2. Erick Erikson, "The Impeachment of Samuel Chase," *Vote for Judges,* March 28, 2005, <http://voteforjudges.blogspot.com/2005/03/impeachment-of-samuel-chase.html> (May 25, 2006).

3. James Mann Art Farm, "John Fries Rebellion Parts

I and II," *James Mann Art Farm,* 2005, <http://www.jamesmannartfarm.com/friesreb1.html> and <http:www.jamesmannartfarm.com/friesreb2.html> (June 8, 2006).

4. "Roger B. Taney," *The Oyez Project,* n.d., <http://www.oyez.org/oyez/resource/legal_entity2> (June 25, 2006).

5. "Supreme Court of the United States," *Microsoft Encarta Online Encyclopedia,* 2006, <http://encarta.msn.com/encyclopedia_761574302_5/Supreme_Court_of_the_United_States.ntml#howtocite> (June 25, 2006).

6. Robert A. Carp and Ronald Stidham, *The Federal Courts* (Washington, D.C.: Congressional Quarterly Press, 1998), p. 9.

7. "The Burger Court: 1969–1986," *The Supreme Court Historical Society,* 2006, <http://www.supremecourthistory.org/02_history/subs_history/02_c15.html> (June 23, 2006).

8. *Washington Post Weekly Review,* October 1, 1984, p. 33.

9. "The Current Court," *The Supreme Court Historical Society,* 2006, <http://www.supremecourthistory.org/02_history/subs_current/02_b.html> (June 13, 2006).

Chapter 4. Important People in the Courts

1. Scott D. Gerber, "Chief Justice Roberts and the Misguided Call of Judicial Pay Raises," January 5, 2006, <http://jurist.law.pitt.edu/forumy/2006/01/chief-justice-roberts-and-misguided.php> (June 28, 2006).

2. "Presidential Impeachment Proceedings," *The History Place,* 2000, <http://www.historyplace.com/unitedstates/impeachments/index.html> (June 20, 2006).

3. "John Jay," *Infoplease,* 2000, <http://www.infoplease.com/ce6/people/A0826053.html> (June 28, 2006).

4. George Will, "Marshall's Legacy," *Washington Post,* September 25, 2005, <http://www.townhall.com/opinion/columns/georgewill/2005/09/25/155697.html> (June 15, 2006).

5. "Taney, Roger Brooke," *Infoplease,* June 29, 2006, <http://www.infoplease.com/ce6/people/A0847779.html> (June 25, 2006).

6. Bernard Schwartz, *A History of the Supreme Court* (New York: Oxford University, 1993), pp. 203–224.

7. "The Justices of the Supreme Court," *InfoSynthesis,* 2005, <http://www.usscplus.com/info/justices.htm> (June 12, 2006).

8. Robert A. Carp and Ronald Stidham, *The Federal Courts,* third ed. (Washington, D.C.: Congressional Quarterly Press, 1998), p. 32.

9. "Guide to Judicial Clerkship," *Indiana University School of Law,* n.d., <http://indylaw.indiana.edu/career/judicialclerkship.htm#why#why> (June 29, 2006).

Chapter 5. What Does the Judiciary Do Today?

1. Felix Frankfurter, "The Supreme Court and the Public," *Forum 83* (June 930: 332.

2. "Originalism," *reference.com,* 2001, <http://www.reference.com/browse/wiki/Originalism> (June 26, 2006).

3. Check Henning, *Wit and Wisdom* (Golden: Colo.: Fulcrum, 1989), p. 250.

4. Thomas R. Dye, L. Tucker Gibson, Jr., and Clay Robinson, *Politics in America* (Upper Saddle River, N.J.: Pearson/Prentice Hall, 2005), p. 384.

5. Ibid.

Blue, Rose and Corinne J. Nadine. *Dred Scott: Person or Property?* Tarrytown, N.Y.: Benchmark Books, 2005.

———. *Marbury v. Madison: The Court's Foundation.* Tarrytown, N.Y.: Benchmark Books, 2005.

Gold, Susan Dudley. *Brown v. Board of Education: Separate but Equal?* New York: Benchmark Books, 2005.

Horn, Geoffrey M. *Thurgood Marshall.* Milwaukee, Wis.: World Almanac Library, 2004.

Jones, Brenn. *Learning About Equal Rights From the Life of Ruth Bader Ginsburg.* New York: Rosen Pub. Group/PowerKids Press, 2002.

Kallen, Stuart A. *John Marshall.* Edina, Minn.: ABDO Pub., 2001.

McElroy, Lisa. *Sandra Day O'Connor: Supreme Court Justice.* Brookfield, Conn.: Millbrook Press, 2003.

McElroy, Lisa Tucker. *John G. Roberts, Jr.: Chief Justice.* Minneapolis: Lerner Publications, 2007.

O'Connell, Kim A. *William Howard Taft.* Berkeley Heights, N.J.: MyReportLinks.com Books, 2003.

Patrick, *John J. The Supreme Court of the United States: A Student Companion.* Oxford; New York: Oxford University Press, 2001.

Weidner, Daniel. *The Constitution: The Preamble and the Articles.* Berkeley Heights, N.J.: Enslow Publishers, 2002.